A HERO ON MOUNT ST. HELENS

A HERO ON
MOUNT
ST. HELENS

THE LIFE AND LEGACY OF
DAVID A. JOHNSTON

MELANIE HOLMES

FOREWORD BY
JEFF RENNER

**UNIVERSITY OF
ILLINOIS PRESS**
Urbana, Chicago, and Springfield

Library of Congress Control Number: 2019936693
ISBN 978-0-252-08431-7 (paper)
ISBN 978-0-252-05134-0 (e-book)

Dedicated to Pat,

and to those who climb mountains,

be it Everest, or peaks formed of challenges and dreams

CONTENTS

FOREWORD

JEFF RENNER

A VOLCANIC CRATER IS A HELLISH PLACE. It can also be a place of beauty, fascination, and awe. David Johnston knew both aspects, and he was among the few who could offer a rich introduction to such an environment. I was fortunate to join David and two of his colleagues in late 1978 when they climbed into the crater of Washington's Mount Baker volcano. Standing 10,781 feet tall, the volcano's heavily glaciated flanks serve as a beacon for the rugged North Cascades near the U.S.-Canadian border. Mount Baker had shown signs of reawakening in 1975, and the team to which David belonged was conducting a scientific assessment of the volcano. I was documenting their work as a science reporter for KING-Television in Seattle and had learned the rudiments of mountain climbing to prepare for this assignment.

The silent snowy beauty of the volcano's upper slopes gave way to the deafening roar of steam from vents called fumaroles as we descended into Mount Baker's crater. Surrounding those vents were gaudy deposits of yellow and orange. "The yellow is sulfur and the orange is a compound of arsenic," explained David. Then he grinned and said, "That's why we wear gas masks when we get close." It was obvious that what I found intimidating was second nature to David. He methodically conducted his research, but with no more drama than if he were preparing breakfast. He took the time to explain the significance of each test to me. His confidence erased my unease, his obvious enthusiasm infectious.

Just a year and a half later, David and I reconnected. Not at Mount Baker, but at Mount St. Helens. A shallow earthquake on March 20, 1980, was the first suggestion that 123 years of silence at the volcano was ending. Seven days later, a steam explosion opened a crater at the summit, blackening the surrounding snowfield with a smudge of ash. As I prepared to fly to the volcano, I telephoned the University of Washington Seismology Lab, seeking a scientist to accompany us in our helicopter. I was pleased the scientist that volunteered was David. During our flight south from Seattle, he provided background on Mount St. Helens's volcanic history and threat. After surveying the volcano from the air, we landed on a nearby ridge. There, David compared Mount St. Helens to a keg of dynamite and said, "The fuse is lit, but we don't know how long it is." And after a brief pause: "If it were to explode right now, we would die."

In the ensuing weeks during the spring of 1980, I came to know David better. My respect for him deepened; our acquaintanceship became friendship. I discovered that I had spent part of my boyhood just miles from his hometown in suburban Chicago. We were two midwestern "boys" who had moved to the Pacific Northwest, embracing every opportunity to spend time in the mountains, though David was far more accomplished in that environment than I.

David expressed two goals in our conversations: improving the scientific understanding and ability to monitor explosive volcanoes such as Mount St. Helens, and raising public understanding of the risks. The hazard assessment based on the ensuing research prompted officials to set up a restricted "Red Zone." But pressure mounted from local property owners, some of whom dismissed the science and maintained they had a right to use their property when and how they wished. The governor bowed to their demands, opening the zone to supervised visits beginning May 17. I reported as residents entered the Red Zone to check on their homes and retrieve belongings. More residents were to enter the Red Zone the next morning on May 18, but the volcano erupted just eighty-eight minutes before the scheduled visit. After spending hours flying in what was called the blast zone, my KING-TV colleagues and I landed to prepare for one of many live broadcasts. Shortly before going on the air, my engineer handed me a piece of paper. "The latest estimate of presumed dead," he whispered. Then: "I'm told we'll recognize some of the names." I later learned David Johnston was on the list.

As I sought brief rest from the sensory and emotional overload that night, I realized that if the volcano had erupted just a little while later, the death toll would have been much higher.

Today, with the perspective of decades of experience as a science journalist and meteorologist, I am struck by the parallels between the debates over the proper response to Mount St. Helens and to the more recent hazard of climate change. We hear the same words now that we heard in 1980. "I don't believe it." "It's junk science." Or, "It's just a theory." (Never mind that a *theory* is peer-reviewed, accepted science, such as gravity.) I believe Mount St. Helens offers lessons today as we confront new environmental hazards, lessons we ignore at our peril.

This book tells the fascinating life story of a scientist who saw it as his duty to remain at his post, close to a volcano he had characterized just two months earlier as a keg of dynamite. David is an icon for all dedicated scientists, most who labor in relative obscurity, but who do so with passion and honesty and excellence.

ACKNOWLEDGMENTS

David Johnston's sister Pat gave permission for this book to be written. She is the sole survivor of a family of five—her parents, Alice and Tom; her brother, David; and an infant sister, Polly, are gone. Thank you, Pat, for letting us pull back the curtain to see the boy whose humble beginnings began with you and your family.

This repository of stories comes from those who opened their hearts and shared memories. More than one hundred people contributed to this book in some way—from around the country and the world. If the four binders of letters and clippings compiled by David's parents are included in the number of people "reached," then that number is much larger. Many words came from beyond the grave, including from David's own writings—the diary he kept as a teenager, as well as letters he wrote from faraway places.

The older generation of David's family is gone except for an elderly aunt, one with a lovely Irish brogue who could offer only a few words about David's dad and what fun "the cousins" used to have. I relied on his sister, a cousin, friends from his childhood and college years, mentors, colleagues, and many others. Understanding the milieu in which David grew meant sifting through thousands of pages of research—about wars, historical events, medical conditions, and above all earth science. I interacted with most of the main contacts who were at Mount St. Helens when David was killed; one died in 2009—Rocky Crandell (who, like David, grew up in Illinois, and like Tom Johnston, lost his only son). A tour of the St. Helens area also helped immensely.

I knew of David and Pat's mother, Alice, through my employment at GSA (General Services Administration, not the Geological Society of America). By coincidence, out of forty-five floors of the Kluczynski Federal Building in downtown Chicago, Alice and I worked on the same floor—on the same side of that floor—so that I saw her almost daily in a break room where she sat with a book in one hand, a cigarette in the other, and a friendly but reserved smile to acknowledge anyone who passed by.

In another coincidence, David's sister Pat lived two blocks from where I moved as a transplant from a small farm town to the Chicago suburbs. I had left my job at GSA to stay home full-time with my two children; shortly thereafter, I wandered my neighborhood, saw Pat and her toddler son in their yard, and asked if our sons might play together. (Thank you, Pat, for saying yes.) She was seven months pregnant at the time with her second son, and my second son was a newborn, nestled in his stroller. It was months into a newly formed friendship before I realized the connection between Pat and her mother, and their shared tragic loss. And it was decades before Pat and I had more than perfunctory words about her brother, because friends don't shine a light into areas that need privacy in order to heal—there were enough people doing that already. So it was a fluke that this book came to be written. When I suggested that her son write about his uncle, I learned it was not in his wheelhouse—then Pat uttered three words: "Why don't you?" I was astounded, flattered, and hesitant. I wondered how it would impact our friendship. The first dinner where we talked about David began tentatively; we were both nervous. She laughed as she talked of her brother's antics; her eyes sparkled. It was a good beginning and we went forward from there.

The science and details in the chapters about Mount St. Helens were reviewed—in part or whole—by Tom Casadevall, Peter Lipman, Dan Miller, Willie Scott, Barry Voight, and Richard Waitt, all of whom were there in 1980; special thanks to each one.

Cindy DiTiberio edited the initial draft of this manuscript; her insight at the onset was invaluable. There were also unofficial editors; they know who they are.

ACKNOWLEDGMENTS

If not for James Engelhardt at University of Illinois Press, this book would not exist in its present form. Every writer asks, *More edits?* With each rendition, the book became better. Thank you, James, for your expertise, patience, and upbeat, supportive words—*Huzzah!*

And to others at UIP (or through UIP) who helped bring out this book—from peer reviewers to production and marketing folks to those who gave endorsement quotes, including Jeff Renner, who wrote the foreword—thank you.

Special thanks to Carolyn Driedger and those on my tour of the CVO in 2016. Thanks also to Rich Batson, Fay Blackburn, Mindy Brugman, Chris Carlson, Cynthia Dusel-Bacon, John Ewert, Lee Fairchild, Anne Glicken, Wes Hildreth, Rick Hoblitt, Joe Jakupcak, Janine Krippner, Doug Lalla, Steve Malone, Marti Miller, Don Mullineaux, Oscar Moore, Chris Newhall, Alyson Newquist, John Pallister, Don Swanson, and Bob Swedko. Gratitude is conveyed posthumously to Stewart McCallum. Thanks also to Angela Boss, Danielle Crabtree, Mary Socki, and Erin Reynolds, as well as Jim Lewis with Menlo Park Historical Association; Cate and Dolly with Oak Lawn Park District; and those at University of Washington who researched fellowship records. There were others, too many to name, that answered my requests for information; each nudged this project forward.

Also, thanks to Judy Pazdan who gave me respite when I faced multiple writing deadlines (thanks most of all for your friendship).

To my mom, who taught through example to love without qualification, to read with vigor, to accept "what is" as well as "what can be." To my kids, thank you for walking with me in the mountains and spending nights in forests. And remember: I like you always; love you forever. A special shout-out to my eldest, whose graphic artistry contributed to this book.

Personal and profound thanks to my rock, Rob, whose support is solid; your belief in me makes all the difference. ILYF&A.

WE ARE ALL ORDINARY. WE ARE ALL SPECTACULAR.
WE ARE ALL SHY. WE ARE ALL BOLD.
WE ARE ALL HEROES. WE ARE ALL HELPLESS.
IT JUST DEPENDS ON THE DAY.

Brad Meltzer

INTRODUCTION

DAVID JOHNSTON WOULD NOT THINK HIS LIFE warranted a book. He didn't think he was special, even though others recognized how remarkable he was. Attracting attention was something he actively avoided. He was shy by nature and abhorred pretentious shows of self-importance. He didn't even use the title Dr., though he almost lost his life in pursuit of his PhD.

Dave came of age in the turbulent 1960s, a time when danger followed people around like their own shadows. The Cold War brought nuclear bomb drills into classrooms and homes, and young men saw Vietnam in their futures.

As a boy, Dave wanted to be like John Glenn—the first American to orbit Earth. When Glenn completed the Friendship 7 mission in 1962, he showed that the United States was a competitor in the space race with the Soviet Union. Glenn was a hero in the eyes of many—the crux of the space race was protection from nuclear attack.

As a man, Dave left his mark on the world through his work in the field of geology. More important, and this is what his family is most proud of, he left an indelible imprint on the hearts of those who knew him.

Almost four decades after his death, hundreds of thousands have spoken David Johnston's name because his story is inextricably intertwined with the most studied volcano in history—Mount St. Helens. His comments, captured by the news media, are bookends for the events that occurred in spring 1980. As the mountain heated up, he compared it to a dynamite keg with its fuse lit; and when it erupted, he saw its beginning from an observation post and shouted into his radio, "This is it!"

Through serendipity, Dave was the first volcanologist on the mountain's flanks when it stirred in March 1980 after its 123-year dormant period. In a news interview, he stood at a viewing area two miles from the summit of the seismically active volcano and told reporters that if it erupted at that moment, they would all die. His statements reflected a healthy fear and deep respect for the dangers of an explosive volcano that he knew all too well—he had narrowly escaped an eruption on a remote Alaskan island four years earlier.

Dave stayed on at Mount St. Helens after that first media interview. He was a U.S. Geological Survey employee hired to expand volcanic gas research in the Cascade Range, of which Mount St. Helens is a part. Since volcanic eruptions are fundamentally gas-driven phenomena, he was not only absorbed by the volcano, he felt an obligation to be there.

Fifty-two days after his "lit fuse" comment, Dave saw the dynamite explode. He was asked to camp overnight at an observation post for a twelve-hour period; that small window turned out to be the last hours of his life. The volcano erupted and destruction stretched much farther than anticipated. Dave was killed on the ridge that now bears his name.

Lodge owner Harry R. Truman died in the eruption. Photographer Dave Crockett lived; as did shopkeeper Stan Lee. Thousands could have perished if not for the persistence of a team of scientists and law enforcement and emergency officials who toiled to protect the area. The official death toll was fifty-seven souls.

Dave would shy away from the limelight and say, "I was doing my job." We hear this from people who serve in the line of fire; they feel anyone would do the same if placed in their situation. Dave was part of a team of geologists tasked with monitoring an active volcano at a time before the science existed to warn of an impending eruption. People with passion so deep, their own safety was compromised as they searched for answers.

The United States had a volcano hazards program at the time but its reach was limited. No volcano observatory existed in the Cascade Range, so when

Mount St. Helens started rumbling, Geological Survey scientists flew in from all over and set up a makeshift office in Vancouver, Washington.

The 1980 eruption brought death and destruction, and it also afforded a seismic shift in the understanding of explosive volcanoes. Research projects—before and after the eruption—are puzzle pieces that formed the big picture. The resulting maturation of volcanology benefits all succeeding generations; it has saved thousands of lives and continues to do so.

People have heard of volcanologist Dr. David A. Johnston who died at Mount St. Helens on May 18, 1980, at 8:32 a.m. (PDT). What they haven't heard are the stories about Dave Johnston, the son, the brother, the friend, whose life spanned thirty years and five months to the day. He did a lot of living in that time. The beginning and middle parts of his life are shared here for the first time thanks to his family and many others. The timing is right for this book. Many of Dave's friends are close to or have entered retirement—although it's not clear whether volcanologists actually retire. They seem to love what they do too much to ever stop. Those whose voices are included herein have helped paint a picture of Dave in all his kind, intelligent, sometimes less-than-perfect hues.

Before the tragedy that took his life, Dave surmounted many personal struggles. The youngest and smallest among his peers, he suffered from low self-esteem. He didn't like that he lagged behind and he chastised himself endlessly. Too often, he didn't feel good enough. His anxious disposition didn't help matters.

Dave eventually found his niche. One that included hard work and sweat and courage and sometimes tears. Although he encountered distress along the way, almost every person who remembers Dave comments on his smile or laughter. A close friend called him "the most unjaded person I ever met." Others admired his childlike curiosity and enthusiasm. These all point to a spark that came from within him—something that helped him overcome many hurdles.

Although Dave's death may appear to be the end, his legacy lives on—one that is much larger than any one person knew until these tales were threaded together. Any book about Dave must honor others besides him; it is what he would want. It is appropriate to recognize heroism in its many forms.

A SHIP IN HARBOR IS SAFE,
BUT THAT IS NOT WHAT SHIPS ARE BUILT FOR.

John A. Shedd

PART ONE

THE WONDER YEARS

THE BOOK OF NATURE IS THE BOOK OF FATE.
SHE TURNS THE GIGANTIC PAGES, LEAF BY LEAF,
NEVER RETURNING ONE.

Ralph Waldo Emerson

TORNADO!

DAVID JOHNSTON WAS SEVENTEEN when a killer tornado raked across his hometown of Oak Lawn, Illinois. Ranked an F4, the tornado killed thirty-three people, injured five hundred, and left six hundred homeless. At one point, the tornado cut a path almost one city block wide and passed a mile from the Johnston home where Dave and two other family members were inside. They were unaware of the nearby danger because it was a time before tornado sirens sang out warnings. It was before the weather service developed an efficient communication system to alert the public. And it was before advancement of radar technology increased the lead time for notification.

Before the progress that we take for granted today, on April 21, 1967, Oak Lawn was caught in a tempest of epic proportion. And it left its mark—on Dave, on his family, and on everyone else involved in the destruction and its aftermath.

The year 1967 conjures images of nature's danger for those who lived in the Chicago area at the time. It started with a record-setting blizzard on January 26. Snow began falling at 5:00 a.m. and continued for twenty-eight hours, blanketing northeast Illinois with twenty-three inches of snow. Sixty people died in the blizzard's wake.[1]

Then in April, ten tornadoes raked across the same area of Illinois, of which three were rated F4. Sixty more lives were extinguished. More than one thousand people were injured. Hundreds were rendered homeless.[2]

The Oak Lawn tornado was one of the three F4s that struck on April 21, and it remains the deadliest tornado recorded in northern Illinois. It crossed a swath of the busiest part of Oak Lawn, where the greatest loss of life occurred that day. After it swept through the village, it continued northeast, clipped Hometown, Evergreen Park, and Chicago's Beverly neighborhood (the only F4 to hit Chicago in recorded history).

The other two F4 tornadoes caused fatalities in Belvidere (near the Illinois–Wisconsin border) and in Lake Zurich. Elementary school kids in Belvidere were already on school buses and high schoolers were lined up outside ready to board. When the tornado hit, students were flung into a muddy field like rag dolls. Twelve buses were rolled like toy Lincoln Logs. Thirteen fatalities and three hundred injuries occurred at Belvidere High School alone.

In Oak Lawn, the term *Black Friday* was about to assume a new meaning. After a long winter and cold wet spring, Chicagoland welcomed a string of 70-degree April days—a real treat for those with cabin fever. However, the weather system ushered in conditions conducive to tornado outbreaks.

Friday, April 21, started out warm and clear in Oak Lawn. Later that day, at the height of evening rush hour, the weekend was unfolding. Motorists swarmed the roadways, shoppers filled the supermarket, and patrons warmed the stools of the local tavern. Kids skated at the roller rink. Many others were outdoors, including Dave, who would have gone for his daily jog. He'd joined his high school's cross-country team and made running a religious practice.

Dave's sister Pat Johnston was also outside, traipsing around the neighborhood. Their mom, Alice Johnston, was running for the Board of Trustees of Moraine Valley Community College (a brand-new local school) and fourteen-year-old Pat was asked to deliver election fliers. However, the ferocious weather drove Pat indoors. She returned home, unable to complete the assigned task.

As a high school senior, Dave typically spent weekends with his buddies or taking pictures of local sporting events for the newspaper where his mother worked as an editor. Dave wasn't one to date in high school. In fact, when senior prom came around, he and his friends—all without dates—went on a weekend campout. On this typical Friday evening, after finishing his run, Dave was in his room. Perhaps he was studying for final exams that were around the corner. One thing for sure, he was unaware that the darkening sky and quickening wind spelled peril.

It was tragic timing—5:26 p.m. People on their way home from work were unaware of the monster about to bear down. At a very busy intersection, Southwest Highway and Ninety-Fifth Street, motorists stuck at the traffic light were caught up in the tornado's fury. Eighteen people were killed at that location.[3] More than twenty-five cars were hurled hundreds of feet. Some sailed hundreds of yards and landed on the north side of Oak Lawn High School; the school sat on the intersection's northwest corner.[4]

Amazingly, no Oak Lawn High School students or school personnel were killed. However, a group of swimmers had a close brush; they vacated the high school pool just thirty minutes prior to the collapse of its roof. The high school sustained $1.5 million in damage (1967 dollars)—but its occupants were lucky— very lucky indeed.

Down the road, the tornado blew out a supermarket's front windows. Its roof caved in and crushed people inside—the youngest victim just eighteen months old. Then the tornado slammed into the Oak Lawn Roller Rink where three more were killed—two kids and one adult. Many others were severely injured, including Dirk Mooth, then eighteen.

Mooth recalled the scene decades later: "We were first aware that something was happening when it became very dark outside and the pressure changes caused my ears to pop. We all stopped what we were doing and looked around when the wind outside began picking up gravel (or debris) from the parking lot and sent it crashing through the windows. We dove for cover. . . . As the storm hit, the noise was unbelievable. I was knocked unconscious. . . . I came to as rain beat down on me. I looked up and saw the sky."[5] Two of Mooth's skating partners died that day—one was thirteen years old, the other fourteen.

Fifteen-year-old Catherine Zenner was caught outdoors and killed when the tornado hit the deadly intersection of Southwest Highway and Ninety-Fifth Street. A petite brunette with a pageboy haircut, Catherine sat near Pat during school lunch period. And Catherine's older sister, Cheryl, was in Dave's class. All attended Harold L. Richards High School in Oak Lawn—a consolidated high school with kids from neighboring towns. Cheryl and Dave were looking forward to graduation. They could not have imagined the carnage that would punctuate the end of their senior year.

Survivors agree that there was no warning. Just a darkening sky that suddenly turned green and the horrific wind that became eerily still.

At the Johnston home were Dave, Pat, and their father, Tom Johnston. None of them were watching television as Chicago weatherman Harry Volkman reported that two tornadoes had hit suburbs north of Chicago just before 4:00 p.m. and at 5:00 p.m. The next report included a sighting near Oak Lawn. Then televisions went dark. Seconds later, the storm hit.

One person remembered an Oak Lawn police squad car drove down Southwest Highway; its loud speaker boomed, "A tornado is in the area; take cover immediately."[6] This mode of warning was well-intended but clearly not effective. Not with a mile-wide F4 tornado on the attack. For many, all they heard was what sounded like a train engine roaring overhead.

After Pat was forced to discontinue her trek around the neighborhood, she called a friend to chat about a school dance that evening. Midconversation, Pat's friend said that she could see a tornado in the distance. Pat's response was, "You're kidding." But the friend wasn't. The Johnstons never sought shelter even though they were a mere mile from the damage path. If the tornado had swerved a bit farther south, they would have been caught up in it.

Dave's mother was still at the office; she worked as an editor of the regional south suburban newspaper. By the time Alice learned of the disaster and phoned home, parts of Oak Lawn were a war zone. Perhaps she asked Tom to go out and see just how bad it was, because Tom quickly ushered Dave and Pat into the car. He drove to a spot about a block from the tornado's path and parked. He ordered his kids to stay put, then he went into the streets alone. Tom wasn't gone long when he returned, visibly shaking, and said, "I can't let you see this," and drove them all home. At that time, Dave earned money as an amateur photographer; he was also about to pursue a photojournalism degree at college. But Tom knew it wasn't a time for photography; it was a time for rescue—and retrieval of bodies.

Dave and Pat didn't realize the gravity of the situation. They thought perhaps their father was acting a bit "melodramatic," as Pat put it. Tom and Alice Johnston practiced the art of shielding their children from displays of anxiety when possible. They downplayed drama in a world that felt riddled with angst—it was their armor against news of the Cold War, Vietnam, assassinations, and bloody clashes in the streets. However, a tornado in their backyard was impossible to minimize. Dave and Pat soon learned of the helplessness that accompanies such a disaster.

From the point of touchdown, the Oak Lawn tornado traveled sixteen miles and took roughly sixteen minutes before it reached Lake Michigan and whirled out over the large body of water. In the time it takes most people to sip their morning coffee, hundreds of buildings and homes were destroyed and another thousand were damaged.

A tornado can blow up buildings as though bombs swirl within its vortex. Sherwood Forest Restaurant on Ninety-Fifth Street in Oak Lawn was filled with a typical Friday night dinner crowd. With tornado reports (in the north suburbs) on the television and vicious winds outside, employees urged patrons to go down to the restaurant's cellar. One customer decided to stay put—John Haggan. Fifty-one-year-old Haggan died when the building exploded around him. The next day would have been his birthday.

With winds more than 200 miles per hour and pressurized updrafts inside the tornado, vehicles were sucked up and spit out. An eyewitness described the "raining" of cars.

"This is crazy. All the sudden, out of the sky a car falls down in the middle of Ninety-Fifth Street!" Robert Kehe, manager of the Coral Theater, aspired to radio broadcasting and took a tape recorder outside. In his voice recording, which lasted five minutes, he went from a standing spectator to a windblown victim, knocked to the ground by the gale's force. He had to crawl on hands and knees back to the safety of the theater.[7]

At one point, Kehe said, "The sky is so dark. Now it's green. *It's green!* . . . The ground is vibrating . . . hail the size of grapes. . . . Oh my God, I'm right in the middle of it."

Kehe had ushered pedestrians inside and directed a few cars off Ninety-Fifth Street into the theater's parking lot—his actions may have saved lives or prevented injuries. He was one of many heroes that day and in the period that followed—in the aftermath of horror.

A news reporter described Oak Lawn: "It's like something out of a film of Berlin during World War II . . . acres of homes and buildings leveled . . . people walking up and down the street weeping." A trailer park was hit; fifty of its homes were destroyed.

A father worried about his son who was at Oak Lawn High School drove over front lawns to reach him. Once at the school, he was terrified to find stuck on a pole a decapitated body wearing a jacket that looked like his son's. But the body had been thrown from the nearby deadly intersection; it was one of the eighteen people killed there. His son turned up unharmed.

Area police and fire departments were overwhelmed with distress calls. Almost five hundred people were transported to twelve hospitals. Emergency rooms filled up quickly; doctors treated debilitating injuries including broken limbs, hips, and glass ground into bodies. Volunteers came from nearby villages and from as far away as Michigan and Ohio. And one thousand soldiers from the National Guard were activated. But before the cavalry showed up, a radio announcer put out a call for immediate help; those with station wagons were needed to transport survivors or move corpses.[8] The VFW Hall in Oak Lawn had been scheduled to host a dance; instead it became a temporary morgue. An Oak Lawn police officer got his wife and kids to safety, then reported to work and didn't return home for three days.

Alice also worked around the clock. Pat said she didn't see her mom for days after the tornado. Tom described his wife as working "by the story"—the tornado seemed a story without end. The *Suburbanite Economist* printed an article about how their staff worked tirelessly through the night of the tornado to produce a special edition by 10:00 a.m. Alice was listed in the article as one of two staff on hand when the tornado hit. With so many people missing and bodies unidentified, disseminating information was crucial.

Tom kept his kids from the havoc beyond their doors on that Friday evening. He knew downed power lines could cause further harm for those who might go roaming. So he stayed home and made sure his kids did the same. But the next day was another story.

After rumors of looting, Sheriff Joseph Woods gave orders to "Shoot looters on sight," and Oak Lawn was sealed off to nonresidents. This meant Dave and his dad were able to reach areas inaccessible to outsiders. The day after the tornado, father and son roamed the streets to capture an unrecognizable landscape.

Wedding album embedded in tree. Photo credited to David A. Johnston in *Oak Lawn Tornado of 1967*. Used with permission of Kevin Korst.

Dave's comprehension of the situation deepened as he bore witness to the aftermath. As with etchings in fresh concrete, images were carved permanently into his mind. Later in life, Dave would refer to the tornado when he spoke of nature's destructive force.

The storm's brute impact was best captured by film—words were not enough. Thirty-one of Dave and Tom's photographs are included in the 2014 book *Oak Lawn Tornado of 1967*.[9] Although all photos are credited to Dave in the book, some were taken by Tom. The image of a wedding album ripped from the safety of someone's home and deeply embedded in a tree speaks of lives torn apart.

Other pictures show mangled buses from the Suburban Transit Company. Each weighed ten tons, but they were thrown through the air—one landed a half-block away in a resident's front yard. Other snapshots show cars wrapped around the concrete columns of a bridge. Some landed upside down, and one car was completely split apart—the front half ripped from the back. A photo of a store parking lot shows a body completely covered with a blanket; the store's casualties included a young mother and her toddler.

Nature's lessons are frequently learned in retrospect. We often don't know about a hazard until it is too late.

Tornado warnings were banned in America until 1938 because officials thought it would induce panic and cause more harm than good.[10] In the 1950s and '60s, the Weather Bureau issued warnings; however, the use of teletype or telephones to disseminate information was slow and ineffective.

The Emergency Broadcast System was launched in 1963, but tornado alerts via television or radio were still somewhat novel in 1967. This was partly because of prediction capability, which was minimal at the time. Also, telephone lines jammed in an emergency, which kept warnings from reaching the airwaves until too late.

Large outdoor sirens existed in 1967, but they were *not* used to warn of tornadoes. Authorized by the Civil Defense Act of 1950, their use was to warn of nuclear attack. Citizens were told, "In case of a raid, the alert will be a warbling siren blast lasting three minutes."

The United States began using sirens to warn of tornadoes in 1970—three years *after* the Oak Lawn disaster. Today, sirens alert those outdoors, and those indoors rely on public radio or television. Also, an NOAA Weather Radio can awake slumbering occupants in case of nocturnal tornadoes. (NOAA offers a free app for smart phones.)

People from rural areas of south-central and midwestern America know that a tornado can darken a clear blue sky like a total solar eclipse. People who survive are those who don't waste time; they seek cover immediately.

Extensive scientific research on tornados has improved forecasting. Now the public has more warning when danger approaches: in 1990, people were typically given five minutes to find shelter; by 2016, that amount increased to fourteen minutes. These improvements are due to superior radar capabilities and better computer models, which allow for enhanced areal identification and more accurate targeting of locations.

Before April 21, 1967, Oak Lawn had no frame of reference for the devastation a tornado could wreak. One witness, who was ten years old at the time, said five decades later that he has thought of the tornado every day since. Those who survived the 1980 eruption of Mount St. Helens have also expressed this sentiment—the experience is forever at the edge of their minds.

For Dave, seeing a tornado rip apart his hometown at a time when the science and communication systems didn't exist to give forewarning likely planted a seed that lay dormant. He started college soon after that April day; however, his study focus was already chosen. Photojournalism—a path his parents had helped open for him.

Even though he didn't immediately pursue the science of the earth's processes, he eventually found his way there. And thirteen years after a killer tornado sideswiped his life, Dave was at the forefront of protecting civilians from a different kind of natural disaster—the deadly blast of a volcano. He likely recalled the inability of officials to warn those in harm's way in Oak Lawn, and it bolstered his courage to speak up about the dangers he saw at Mount St. Helens.

FAMILY, WHERE LIFE AND LOVE BEGIN.

Anonymous

2

THE JOHNSTON FAMILY

DAVE LOOKED UP TO HIS DAD. In fact, he thought highly of all those who had served their country. On Veterans Day 1965, when Dave was fifteen, he wrote, "I owe a good deal to the men, which includes my own father, to whom this day is dedicated."

At twenty-six, he felt patriotism at a broader level. It was 1976, America's bicentennial, and Dave wrote, "Yesterday, the bicentennial was a bumper-sticker and a candy wrapper, but today it is my mother, my grandfather, Ken Gooley.* . . . I feel very proud today of my heritage, I'm not blind to its faults . . . but I believe that the U.S. has given an opportunity to man/woman/kind to learn what life must be in order to have meaning. . . . Everything America is, was, and ever will be is the result of what its people are."

Tom Johnston stood for America when he fought in World War II. Never one to talk about his service, he stashed away his stories—stored on pieces of paper, carefully typewritten, double-spaced, by a young Tom's hand—to be discovered many years later by his daughter. At nineteen, he took part in fifteen bombing missions over Japan from April through July 1945 with the U.S. Air Force.

---

* Kenneth Gooley was Dave's childhood friend who served during Vietnam.

Tom and Alice Johnston with their children Dave and Pat, December 1957. Photo courtesy of Johnston family.

"Mission One" was on April 24; the intended target was an aircraft plant fourteen miles west of Tokyo. Tom wrote,

> We had a normal take-off and uneventful trip to the Jap mainland. We arrived at the assembly point . . . spotted our lead, formed up and headed to the target. . . . We appeared tense, excited and a little scared. We began to pick up flak the minute we hit the coast. . . . This was the first flak I have seen except in movies. The next several minutes we were over the mountains and saw no flak. Mount Fujiyama was beautiful, all covered with snow on top and down the sides, like a picture post card. . . . As we neared the target we began to get heavier flak. . . . The bomb bay doors were open and we started on our bomb run. At this point the formation flies straight and level with no course changes. This is when the planes are sitting ducks. We went over the target and the lead crew dropped their bombs and the rest of the formation followed suit. The sky was filled with bombs, an unforgettable sight. . . . The lead plane was hit in the aft-end with an anti-aircraft shell. It was a direct hit . . . the tail section was blown away from the main part of the plane, flipped upside down and plunged into the target area. I prayed to see chutes, there were none. . . . I lost all sense of feeling.

After a mission in June, Tom wrote, "Passing over the mainland and out to sea, we could look back and see three cities in flames. From 14,000 feet, it was beautiful in a horrible, horrible way. How much more can they stand?"

Not long after this mission, President Harry S. Truman authorized use of the world's first atomic bomb, dropped on Hiroshima on August 6, 1945. And another was dropped on Nagasaki on August 9. Six days later, Japan unconditionally surrendered, ending World War II.

Tom looked the part of an Irishman with bright red hair. His immigrant parents were born and raised in Ireland. They came to America around 1910 and settled on the south side of Chicago in an area populated by others of Irish descent. Tom was the youngest of four children born to George and Adeline Johnston. Then in 1934 in the midst of the Great Depression, when Tom was just nine years old, his dad died.

The family of working-class immigrants pulled together. Tom's three older siblings lived at home and held jobs. Adeline took in laundry and cleaned houses. And that Christmas, Tom went to the local grocer to see about odd jobs. Knowing the boy had lost his father, the owner put him to work, then sent him home with twenty dollars. Adeline Johnston cried when she saw the money. For the rest of his life, Tom could recall every item purchased with that small windfall.

While Tom grew up in a large close-knit family with aunts and uncles and lots of cousins, this was not Alice Ward's experience. Her mother, Ruth Metcalfe, was an only child, and Alice's three maternal great-aunts were single; none had children. This resulted in a dearth of extended family. Also, like Tom, Alice lost her father at a young age—but not to death.

Alice's heritage was mainly English; her ancestors came to America very early—some before the Revolutionary War. She was sandwiched between two brothers, Dudley (one year older) and Arthur (three and a half years younger, called "Artie"). Her parents William and Ruth Ward lived with their kids in Antioch, a far north Chicago suburb that touched Wisconsin's border.

Advanced education for women of Ruth Metcalfe's generation was not common, but her family sent her to the University of Chicago, where she earned a degree in home economics. It is there that she met William Ward, her future husband, who was fresh out of the military, having served in World War I. Ruth and William were married around 1925. A census in 1940 listed William as a salesman in the "Breweries" industry—it would be the last census that showed the family intact. It turned out that alcohol was part of William's home life as well as his work life. After about sixteen years, three kids, and a whole lot of alcohol, discontent drowned the Wards' marriage.

Alice would have been about thirteen when her dad left the state and started a second family. Armed with the degree she had earned, Ruth found an office job in downtown Chicago at Montgomery Ward, a retail department store. It was then that life at home for Alice and her brothers became "hell"—Alice's assessment—because the bitterness of abandonment fueled Ruth's own alcohol abuse and kept her from mothering her children well. By the time Alice earned her high school diploma, she was ready to bolt. A friend's family offered to take her in, but she didn't want to be a burden, so she found a job and a roommate and struck out on her own.

Alice was only fifteen when she graduated high school. She had attended a school that combined grades (first and second, third and fourth, and so on), and she'd skipped ahead. She never liked being the youngest among her classmates, but it did afford her an opportunity she would not have had otherwise. World War II still waged when she graduated in 1943, which meant jobs were plentiful in the states—jobs that soldiers had vacated. Alice landed a position at the legendary Pullman Company in Chicago. At one time, Pullman produced 90 percent of the sleeping cars in North America; but train travel declined, especially during the Depression. With World War II came military contracts—train cars were needed to transport troops and guns.[1] This is the time in which Alice began clerking for Pullman's treasurer. After the war, Tom was discharged from the air force and hired as a clerk in Pullman's legal department. The couple met in the halls of their workplace, and after a three-month courtship, they were married in 1947 in a small ceremony. She was nineteen; he had just turned twenty-one.

Not long after the exchange of nuptials, Alice's family ties tugged. Among her three unmarried great-aunts, two had teachers' pensions that supported all three under one roof into old age, including Geraldine, who never worked. This arrangement fell apart when the two income earners died and their pensions disappeared. Then Geraldine needed help. So Alice and Tom moved from their newlywed abode on the north side of Chicago to the home of Alice's great-aunt, Aunt Gerry, in Winnetka—a near-north suburb of Chicago.

It wasn't an ideal living situation. Aunt Gerry had idiosyncrasies that got under Alice's skin. Such as the habit of allowing her cat to carry its kill inside the house and munch on it among family members—including in front of Alice and Tom's children. Both Dave and Pat were born while the Johnstons lived in the cat-kill house. Since Alice didn't have much family, she likely felt a duty to help what little she had. But eventually Aunt Gerry needed round-the-clock care, so the house was sold and the proceeds were completely absorbed by nursing facility fees.

Tom and Alice looked around for a home where they could raise their two children and found the GI Bill a boon because it made low-interest mortgages available to veterans. Hometown, Illinois, drew their attention because it was designed for World War II and Korean War vets. Southwest of Chicago's city limits, it was the largest planned community of its kind.[2] For nonveterans, a down payment for a home was $1,400 (about $14,000 in 2019 dollars); for veterans, just $200. Tom's service enabled them to buy a Hometown abode and a piece of the American dream.

The young family settled into their own home. It was a fresh beginning and trials of the past faded. But another of life's hurdles was thrown into their path. Alice's younger brother, Artie, joined the navy at a time when no war waged. Still, he met a tragic end.

Paper as thin as onion skin tells how Petty Officer Arthur Ward was washed overboard in rough seas and drowned in February 1955. He had just transferred from the USS *Zellars* (DD-777) to the USS *Clarence K. Bronson* (DD-668) before the accident. The ship's commander wrote to Ruth Ward about her son's death: Arthur "was in sight and was swimming well toward us . . . he was about 800 yards away when a heavy sea curled over him and he went down . . . he came back to the surface but was swimming feebly. In less than a minute . . . he stopped moving. Line-throwing guns shot lines within yards of him . . . but he went down and was never sighted again. . . . The time from Man Overboard until we last saw him was 13 minutes." The commander declared Arthur Ward's efforts to swim in the torrential seas "gallant and superhuman."

Alice's photo album held a picture of her twenty-two-year-old brother Artie with four-year-old Dave. A Christmas tree graces the background, and Dave's mouth is puckered, poised to plant a kiss on his Uncle Artie's cheek. Two months later, Artie was gone.

21

Petty Officer Arthur Ward
(Alice's brother). Photo
courtesy of Johnston family.

Dave and his Uncle Artie. Photo
courtesy of Johnston family.

Alice felt her brother's loss acutely; perhaps more so because she came from a small family unit. And as Alice's world shrank, so did her children's. Alice yearned to hear stories about her brother from those who worked with him before he died, but the internet was decades away; there was no way to connect with his shipmates. One day when Alice saw a boat with 777 painted on its side (she remembered the *Zellars*'s hull number), she asked Tom to stop the car. She approached the boat's owner and asked if he'd served in the navy. He had not. Six decades after the drowning, research led to one of Artie's ex-shipmates. The aged former sailor remembered Artie as a boiler technician who worked with the ships' steam propulsion boilers—"a most responsible position."

The family heard only how Artie died in service to his country, the result of nature's fury, and that his body was never recovered—a fate that Dave would meet twenty-five years later. Buried on a mountain ridge. Buried at sea. Both died in the field while serving their country.

Perhaps it is because of the loss of Artie that Alice decided to overlook the past and accept her mother into her home. Even though Ruth had her rough edges, Alice's yearning for family was strong. Ruth moved in with the Johnstons, a situation with a new set of challenges. The Hometown house grew too small, so the family resettled in nearby Oak Lawn—it was there that Dave's young life unfolded.

There were more drawbacks to the living situation than house size. Ruth, called "Gram" by Dave and Pat, lived with the Johnstons for many years and it was not without reverberations. The same problem that cropped up in her years as parent reared its head as grandparent. Because of close proximity, her grandkids observed her bad habit. Dave's diary sums it up. There were visitors to the Johnstons' home and fifteen-year-old Dave wrote, "Gram was inebriated. Dad got angry. Mom cried."

Ruth was not without excuses to self-medicate with alcohol. She was divorced and left to raise three children. She had lost one son to the navy, and the Cold War threatened to snatch her other son, Dudley, who was in the army during the Cuban Missile Crisis.

Dudley, who rarely wrote home, sent a ten-page letter about the dangerous situation when Russia placed nuclear missiles in Cuba in October 1962—aimed at the United States. President John F. Kennedy warned Russia against the placement, just ninety miles from Key West, Florida. The warning was ignored. The Cuban Missile Crisis put the U.S. military at DEFCON 2; war was considered imminent.

After thirteen tense days, the United States agreed to no further invasions of Cuba; then, and only then, did Russia remove its missiles. It is the closest the world has ever come to nuclear war, and Dudley would have been in it. Thankfully, he came home, and brother, sister, and mother were reunited.

Alice was part of the generation of women who held jobs of importance during World War II then heard it was their "patriotic duty" to return home so that men returning from the service could have their jobs back. Alice held her first job at fifteen; she had enjoyed that sense of identity and fulfillment. So even after she was married with children, she actively cultivated a life beyond her home's doors.

In the 1950s, she served in city government as an alderman in Hometown. She landed a newspaper job in the 1960s. And in 1967 when a new community college opened, she received the second-highest number of votes to become a member of the original Board of Trustees—one of eight people elected and the only woman. (She served two additional terms at Moraine Valley Community

College before rotating off the board.) Alice attended women's rights conventions, and family lore has it that she quit an office job when she found she was paid less than a male colleague.

The world of writing proved an accessible outlet for Alice's intellect and energy; she started freelancing for the small *Worth-Palos Reporter* shortly after it was founded in 1960. Eventually she moved up to editor, and it was then that she helped others along the journalism path. Dave had learned photography from his dad; they even had a darkroom in their basement. Alice recruited fifteen-year-old Dave as an amateur photographer for the paper so that he could earn his own money and learn responsibility.

She encouraged another teenage boy toward the role of journalist, one who went on to become a longtime reporter for the historic *Chicago Sun-Times*. Zay Smith did odd jobs around the newspaper office, and Alice used her trademark humor to encourage him. One day she said, "Zay, you're not very good at sweeping, why don't you try your hand at this obituary here?"[3] Years later, Zay remarked on Alice's "wonderful laugh" and said, "As a journalist, she was all business; tough as could be, sensitive but tough. I've worked for several top editors and Alice was one of the best."[4]

Like his wife, Tom was never one to idle his engine. Both Tom and Alice were children of the Depression, and both learned the merits of hard work. Tom landed a job at Chicago's Peoples Gas (a natural gas utility company) with the title of engineer even though he hadn't attended college. He did some fieldwork but most of his time was spent behind a desk.

Outside of work, Tom's time revolved around mentoring youth. He was a scoutmaster and baseball coach, and he volunteered his time for the local park district. One of Dave's childhood friends said that Tom always connected well with the younger generation. Another friend thought of him as a second dad and called late at night for rides home from his job as dishwasher at a local restaurant. Tom was always happy, even eager, to oblige. Not having a father while growing to manhood, he was particularly sensitive to the needs of youth in his sphere. Decades later, the late-night caller talked of Tom and said, "I loved that man."

One of Dave's high school pals described Tom as "military and sort of strict." By high school, Dave began having trouble with math, and Tom was a stickler about grades—he got angry with Dave. Call this strict, call it military, or call it a father butting heads with a son over grades—Dave referred to his dad as having occasional "conniptions." This is likely what the friend remembered. Pat expanded a bit more: "We weren't afraid of my dad, but we knew his rule—he would only say it once. If he had to repeat himself, watch out." She meant that a reprimand, grounding, or extra chores would follow if she or Dave acted up.

In 1959, when Alice was thirty-one, she and Tom were expecting their third child. But expectation of happiness turned to sorrow when little Polly Johnston succumbed to liver failure due to infection a few days after birth.

There are several causes of acute liver infection in a newborn. In Polly's case, it was due to neonatal hemochromatosis—excess iron in the body. The condition was first reported in medical literature in 1957, just two years before her birth. Unlike its counterpart, hereditary hemochromatosis, the cause is not genetic. Six decades later, its exact cause is not understood, but there appears to be a maternal link with a high risk of recurrence in subsequent births.

Neonatal hemochromatosis is the most common cause of liver failure in newborns, and liver transplant is the only known curative treatment. The first transplant was attempted in 1963, but it wasn't until 1967 that a transplant extended survival by more than a few days or weeks. The National Organization for Rare Disorders reports that more research is necessary to understand the disease that caused Polly's death.

With the hope of someday saving others from such heartache, Alice and Tom made a decision, one that may have given a bit of meaning to their daughter's death. They donated her body to science. Many parents would back away from this step. With their hearts broken, Alice and Tom grasped at what little solace they could find.

Dave was nine and in fourth grade when his baby sister died. As the oldest and the big brother, he would have been charged with watching out for his younger sister Pat, and he would have expected to look out for his second sibling too. But he never got the chance—Polly was the sister no one could protect.

Pat was two and a half years younger than Dave, and she had looked forward to becoming a big sister. Her parents prepared her by buying a book about what it's like when a new baby comes home. Still, they didn't give her much information when Polly died. She remembers being told that her parents "lost

25

the baby." Her six-year-old mind reeled, and she wondered, *Why don't they go find it?!*

Gram cautioned Dave and Pat not to talk about Polly because the topic would be hard on their mom and dad. So the family went on, with silence shrouding Polly's death. The pact not to discuss the littlest Johnston lasted well into Pat's adulthood; many decades later, it is information that she doesn't volunteer, even with longtime friends.

Dave and Pat developed a typical sibling relationship with equal measures of love and razzing. This included occasionally tormenting each other. As Pat tells it, "He tied me to a tree so he could steal my bike." Of course the ties weren't tight. She surrendered to his ploy and quickly struggled free. Another day, Pat took Dave's bike without asking; so next time she wanted to borrow it, he made her sign a contract. All's fair in love and bikes it seems.

With age comes big responsibility. Dave took it upon himself to "help" his little sister be more productive with her time. When he thought she watched too much television, he devised a plan. From his bedroom across the hall from the TV room/den, he set up his toy cannon with its barrel aimed at the hallway. When Pat climbed the stairs, intent on reaching the TV room—wham! Little plastic balls stung her legs. It was at times such as these that she thought of her brother as "Evil David."

In retaliation for some of Dave's annoying moments, Pat seized the opportunity to lock him in their home's basement—an area that doubled as a family recreation area and held Pat's collection of vinyl records. Dave quickly came up with an idea—for every thirty seconds that passed, he would break one of her records. She called his bluff. Thirty seconds later, she heard a crash through the door. He had zeroed in on the record he hated most: Tom Jones's *What's New Pussycat?* After listening to Jones croon about a woman powdering her pussycat nose and making up her pussycat eyes, Dave was happy to put an end to its melody.

Yet if anyone else messed with his sister, Dave stepped into the role of protector. When a boy threw rocks at her, he set the young lad straight. Dave had big brother buttons, and when those buttons were punched, he became her armor.

One evening, Dave found himself protecting Pat from their parents' ire. When an adolescent Pat held a party in their basement, there was alcohol and she became tipsy. Dave spent the evening keeping an eye on the party and repeatedly ran upstairs to deliver reports to their parents—all was "fine." When Dave asked Pat what she thought would happen if she got caught, she drew her index finger across her throat and smiled.

Dave didn't judge people who drank. Neither did Alice, even though alcohol was the source of much pain in her life—including her father's death.

Well into adulthood, Alice tracked down her father, reestablished ties, and began mailing him photos of his two grandchildren. But Dave and Pat never got to meet the grandfather who called himself "WW3." Because no sooner had Alice found him than she lost him again when his drinking brought him to a strange and terrible end.

Coming home drunk late one night, William Ward purportedly got confused and tried to enter a neighbor's house instead of his own. He was too drunk to realize his mistake and the resident thought it was an intruder. A warning was shouted, but the confused William only redoubled his efforts to enter. A gunshot rang out. Alice's father was shot through the door and died from the wound. This is the story Alice was told, and it's the one she passed along to her kids—both of whom grew up grandfatherless.

Dave and Pat got to know only one of their grandmothers because Tom's mother, Adeline, also died too soon—she succumbed to cancer when Dave was a preschooler and Pat was a baby. The one grandmother they knew was *not* one to dote. In fact, tension created with Gram in their home was a definite hindrance to harmony.

What Tom and Alice didn't know was that Gram shamed a confused Pat when she asked to read the book one more time about a new baby coming home—*after* Polly's death.

Dave also was unsettled by Gram. He felt she inserted herself where she didn't belong, specifically pertaining to his dog, who already attracted Alice and Tom's ire because of certain behaviors. Dave missed his mom or dad when they took trips, but he admitted that he didn't miss Gram when she was away.

Each person encounters obstacles throughout life. Likewise, every generation has cause for worry. The 1960s brought about an avalanche of anxiety in America. Women demanded their rights to enter previously male-dominated careers and to control their reproductive health. Black Americans struggled for safety, respect, and a voice in politics. The younger generation spouted antiestablishment slogans such as sex, drugs, and rock and roll.

And Americans grew increasingly concerned about their role in a war that seemed endless. From Kennedy to Johnson to Nixon, American presidents accepted the domino theory—that if Vietnam became a communist-led country, all of Southeast Asia would follow suit. Twenty-three thousand military advisors were already in Vietnam before the first ground troops were sent in March 1965. By November 1967, a group called Vietnam Veterans Against the War formed in order to share personal experiences about "troubling battlefield tactics and strategies."[5]

By that time, Dave was in college. With draft registration required at age eighteen, it was one time that being the youngest among his peers worked in Dave's favor. His late birthday meant he entered college at seventeen, and with college—at least at the undergrad level—came a draft deferment.

Much of the time, however, being so much younger than his peers was a source of angst for Dave.

IT WAS THE BEST OF TIMES, IT WAS THE WORST OF TIMES.

Charles Dickens, *A Tale of Two Cities*

3

YOUNGEST AND
SMALLEST

TOM AND ALICE'S KIDS were part of the post–
World War II baby boom—it was a time when America's economy grew at a fast rate. However, peace of
mind was thwarted when war threatened Americans
once again.

The 1948 U.S.-financed Marshall Plan, called the
European Recovery Program, sought to stabilize Eu-
rope and encourage democracy, thereby discouraging
communism. Western European countries enjoyed
economic recovery under the plan, but Russia had
declined participation, and other eastern European
countries followed Russia's lead. In April 1949, NATO
was formed—a military alliance of North American and European nations—and
a few months later the world was shocked when Russia exploded its first atomic
bomb.

Dave at age one and a half.
Photo courtesy of Johnston
family.

Almost as soon as World War II ended, a different kind of war took hold—
the Cold War—one without a handbook for battle. Fear of communism spread
across America. The House Un-American Activities Committee (HUAC) and

the Red Scare were in full swing. In February 1950, Senator Joseph McCarthy accused the State Department of employing fifty-seven card-carrying communists and demanded action by President Truman.[1] Then in June, North Korea, backed by Russia, crossed the arbitrary line drawn at the end of World War II known as the 38th parallel, and the Korean War began. President Truman stated, "The attack upon Korea makes it plain . . . that communism has passed beyond the use of subversion to conquer independent nations and will now use armed invasion and war."

The 1950s was an era of repression and hysteria. Countless Americans were investigated for their links to communism. Hundreds were blacklisted, including athletes, journalists, actors, even dancers—many lives were ruined. Rumors circulated that two actors died of heart attacks due to the stress of being unable to work—Canada Lee, age forty-five, and John Garfield, age thirty-nine, died twelve days apart in May 1952.

While some lives were ruined by HUAC and McCarthyism, other lives were just beginning. Dave was born on December 18, 1949, as a new decade was about to dawn. His late birthday meant he entered first grade almost four months shy of age six. So at age five in fall of 1955, he learned to "duck and cover" in case of a nuclear attack by Russia. He was taught to duck under his desk and cover his head with his arms. The Johnstons along with all Americans were advised by the government to stock food and water in their basements. Fatalism spread, and with it, fallout shelters.[2] This mindset was so pervasive that there were even recommendations by the Toy Guidance Council about which toys were appropriate for shelters. A 1955 article noted, "Toys are supposed to teach children to face situations they'll meet as adults . . . to teach hazards of adult life." The council asked, "Kids may think toys are for play, but what do kids know?"[3]

Tom and Alice witnessed their share of the world's dangers but they did not fashion a fallout shelter in their home. Nor did they stockpile food and "shelter appropriate" toys. They couldn't keep talk of bombs out of their kids' schools but they kept it out of their home.

As a boy, Dave was proud of his middle name—Alexander. Brave and strong, Alexander the Great said, "There is nothing impossible to him who will try." Dave was likely the youngest among his classmates. He was also a late bloomer, which meant he was the smallest.

Because of his small stature, Dave was allowed to fill in for players in younger divisions of the local baseball league and kids thought he was a year or two younger than his actual age. Over time, Dave became his own harshest critic. He chastised himself after, in his own words, "another hitless time at bat while Baird got a double." Dave desperately wanted to catch up with the other boys. He even started working out with weights, hoping to bulk up.

In school, kids like Dave who are among the youngest will at first be behind their older peers in terms of language, motor abilities, and social skills, which can impact confidence. According to educational psychologist Kairen Cullen, "Those early formative years influence attitudes and expectations about success, academically and socially, and that can possibly stay with an individual."[4]

Dave experienced low self-esteem and his confidence lagged. But the extent to which being the youngest influenced him over the long-term isn't necessarily negative because there is another side to this issue. While older elementary students perform better on tests and do better socially, by eighth grade the disparity evens out. And by college, younger students repeatedly outperform older ones in any given year. This reversal in performance arises from the youngest always striving to overcome obstacles in the form of older, more-developed kids. While there's a benefit to being bigger and stronger, younger kids acquire grit—the knowledge that perseverance, dedication, and motivation can help you where an absolute advantage may not come to the rescue.[5]

This is where Dave benefitted from being the youngest. When he perceived that he had failed, such as when his grades lagged and he thought he was a letdown to one of his favorite teachers, he wrote in his diary that he would "try harder."

Because of his small size, Dave sometimes felt left out. He didn't fit in with his peers in gym class or on the ballfield. It didn't help when a classmate made fun of his physique, a common occurrence among adolescent boys, but it hit Dave a bit harder. And with girls, he felt invisible. The result was a decreased sense of belonging—which is a basic need that receives far less attention than it should, according to early childhood educator Ruth Wilson. "The results of not having belonging-needs met are usually serious . . . and this happens only within a social context," wrote Wilson.[6]

Dave got a lot out of being a Boy Scout, including filling his needs to belong and fit in. He even wore his uniform on vacation because he wanted to connect

Dave wearing scout uniform on vacation, with Tom and Pat.
Photo courtesy of Johnston family.

with any fellow scouts he might encounter. Boy Scouts also leveled the playing field for Dave. He enjoyed the sense of accomplishment by earning merit badges. The more badges he earned, the higher he rose in the ranks. He even attended a week-long Junior Leadership Training camp, which gave him authority over some of the lower-ranked scouts in his troop. He rather enjoyed doling out assignments to the other kids.

Another reason Dave benefitted from scouting is rooted in the history of boys' clubs. A precursor of Boy Scouts was the Boys' Brigade, founded in the 1800s; its mission was to promote "all that tends toward true Christian manliness."[7] The brigades organized boys into "quasi-military groups where they camped, learned woodcraft, and performed good deeds in a manly sort of way."[8] The clubs taught survival skills and drilled boys like soldiers in order to teach them to be "men."

For a boy who saw himself as lagging in attributes considered "manly," scouting offered much. Dave stuck with it longer than other boys his age, into his junior year of high school.

The Cold War's next frontier was space, and Dave dreamed of being a part of it. He was aware of America's attempts to catch up with Russia's space program. Russia's launch of Sputnik in 1957 was a show of communism's power. It meant they possessed the capability to deliver a nuclear warhead into American skies. Dave was in eighth grade when John Glenn became the first American to orbit Earth in 1962. After which, he promptly cut out a picture of an astronaut, snipped away the face, and inserted his own photo inside the helmet.

Dave's love of science was fostered by frequent forays into nature. Dave's cousin Rick went with Tom and Dave on camping excursions in upstate Michigan where they would stargaze for hours. Away from the city lights, stars seemed more abundant. The night sky, as well as the boys' heads, teemed with stars. Rick remembers his Uncle Tom setting up the telescope so the boys could see Saturn and its rings.

Outdoor sojourns were some of Dave's happiest times. One day, on a fifteen-mile hike with his scout troop, he discovered a bunch of geodes. Bursting them open revealed the crystals inside. He was fascinated and eager to know how they had formed.

Dave found many ways to quench his keen curiosity—from experimenting with his model volcano to watching the warring armies in his ant farm. Coincidentally, his ant farm was one of the first ways he got to see activity that takes place underground.

Nature trips with his family, friends, and scout troop had other advantages; they assuaged Dave's growing anxiety. When one focuses one's eyes on the horizon for sustained periods, the brain releases endorphins—similar to a runner's high. On those trips, Dave breathed fresh air, and endorphins pinged in parts of his brain that overrode feelings that challenged him. Outdoors, he felt unencumbered.

If Dave had to be indoors, he could be found devouring James Bond books. Or perhaps watching the television show *The Man from U.N.C.L.E.*, with good-guy spies much like 007. Dave loved the idea that bravery and ingenuity prevailed in the face of peril, that there were forces capable of swooping in to save the day.

Dave in white denim jeans, with Pat.
Photo courtesy of Johnston family.

Dave wore white denim jeans as a kid because "good guys wear white"—a direct quote from his younger self per childhood chum Rich Batson. The two grew up on the same block on Ninety-Ninth Place in Oak Lawn and hung out with the same group of boys. Rich remembers Dave as a nice guy. But Dave wasn't always good, such as when he chopped down his grandmother's asparagus plants because, well, he hated asparagus.

But Dave believed that good conquered evil. Like the white hats worn by Roy Rogers and the Lone Ranger to signal their moral purity, Dave's boyhood white denims were symbols of the type of person he wanted to be.

He wanted to be one of the good guys, but eventually he discarded the notion that he needed to wear white to show it.

Days after Dave turned fifteen on December 18, 1964, he received a label maker for Christmas and immediately typed out his personal credo: "You can't waste a day!" Then in a serious tone he turned to his sister and said, "Just think, we'll never get today back again."

Dave's mantra reflected a nugget of truth expressed a couple thousand years earlier when the Roman poet Horace coined the phrase "carpe diem." *Carpe* means "seize, enjoy, or make use of," and *diem* means "day." Dave seemed to understand that each day is a new and unique opportunity, and it is a choice to make the most of each one.

A week later 1964 turned into 1965, and Dave began writing in a black leather-bound diary with a maroon spine. America started 1965 by drafting 5,400 young men to fight in Vietnam; by year's end, more than 45,000 were called to serve.[9] Teenage boys such as Dave saw war on the horizon. About the same time that combat troops first landed in Vietnam—on March 8, 1965—Dave reached the midpoint of his life at fifteen years and two and a half months.

Dave's diary speaks the thoughts of a boy who considered an early demise. A passage reads: "I can't wait for this school year to be over, but just think, what if I die before then?" On a midsummer day, he checked out a book about Vietnam from the library. And as he began his junior year of high school, he stopped by a military recruiting station; his diary entry was: "Even though I'm almost six years early, I want to make plans." Dave wanted to go to college but he felt the war would be waiting when he finished.

The 1960s found Mach 1–busting jets in America's skies. Deployed by the air force, the jets were designed to keep the peace during the Cold War.[10] As the jets soared overhead, sonic booms shook those below—reminders of unseen threats. People who lived near big cities, including Chicago, found sonic booms were everyday occurrences for months at a time.

Dave wrote in his diary that the sonic booms would "start up again soon and continue for months." School days were shattered by sounds that startled him and made his teacher "jump a foot." Researchers documented psychological trauma for a generation of children. A woman said the sound of water reminded her of the noise the jets made and that she was afraid she'd die in the shower.[11] Another person who went to grade school in New York City talked of how it took years to get over the daily fear of instant incineration. More than thirty-eight thousand claims were made against the air force to cover losses caused by sonic booms; among them were stories of pets dying and livestock going insane.

The first page of Dave's 1965 diary lists his new year's resolutions: "(1) I will always do my homework; (2) I will work out regularly; (3) I will earn at least one scouts merit badge per month; (4) I will practice my lessons for band at least every other day; (5) I will not do anything to anyone that I wouldn't want them to do to me." His do-unto-others resolution is illustrated by an entry about a day of ice skating where some kids playing crack the whip "grabbed a girl and dragged her across the ice." Dave thought it was funny at first but wrote, "then I started thinking about it."

Dave started the second half of his sophomore year of high school in January 1965. He dreaded the return to school after the holiday break. Partly because of a problem with public speaking; he wrote, "I had to give a career report. . . . I don't know why, but I felt sick. When I realized that I was getting too upset, I had to sit down to halt the process or it would have ended with me sprawled all over the floor." The other part of school he dreaded was public displays of strength, such as in gym class when boys did pull-up tests. He wrote, "I was helped on the only one I got. I felt ridiculous." His view of himself as inadequate extended into many areas. After playing basketball, he wrote, "I smell at it." After playing tennis: "Boy, was I crummy."

Dave did fairly well in school, although he wrote about being "afraid" during math class—his weakest subject. In March, he wrote, "My entire world is collapsing around me. I got a D-minus on my geometry test. I think I did bad on the biology test yesterday, and hate to think how I did on the German test. . . . I have entered a fatal tail spin. If I don't recover I could ruin my entire life." This melodramatic entry reflects how anxious Dave was about his future. When he took a day-long test, one taken nationwide by all kids his age, he worried that a future employer might want to see it.

When he received two As on English essays, he chalked it up to luck—yet he ended that semester as one of the top ten students in his English class. Overall, he was a B-average student; this included accelerated classes where a B counted for more.

Dave's anxious personality was likely part genetic and part environmental. He found some relief with his dog, Max, a dachshund with a tan coat whose unconditional acceptance was good therapy. Unfortunately, Max had problems,

Dave and his dog, Max. Photo courtesy of Johnston family.

some of which Gram commented on mercilessly. When Max bit a guest, he was quarantined. Shortly thereafter, Dave wrote, "Today was the worst day in 1965 and perhaps in my whole life, aside from family deaths. Today, Mom gave away Max. . . . I'm in a daze. . . . I have to change the subject because I'm crying and beginning to feel ill." Dave blamed himself. He felt he had failed, that he hadn't been responsible or taken good enough care of his dog.

Dave perceived Max's loss as a cosmic injustice and he wrote, "As I think about poor Max . . . I also think, *How could there be a God?*" Perhaps he prayed to a benevolent being and didn't receive the answer he was looking for. But when a neighbor's dog turned up pregnant, Max turned out to be the father and Dave got to pick a new puppy. He chose "the prettiest and smallest"—a male and the runt of the litter. Dave thought having one of Max's puppies might help him feel better, and then he called himself self-centered for trying to get over Max. Unfortunately, the stage was set for repeated loss when Dave was given two months to housebreak his new dog, Sandy. The deadline came and went, and he wrote, "May 19, 1965, was bad for me . . . mom gave away Max

. . . a similar occurrence will soon return me to my dismal feelings. Mom has decided Sandy should go. Ok well, that's what happens when you're not born housebroken and someone else loves you." After the milkman took Sandy home with him, Dave ignored his diary for days. When he caught up, he was "dead tired"—dejection's footprint.

Besides working through adversity, Dave used his diary to practice creative writing—the pages teem with humor. On the kind of midwestern fall day that hints at the cold to come, Dave wrote, "Today I left my day free for whatever I wanted to do. Except my mother made it clear what I wanted to do. I wanted to dig a hole to plant Gram's tree. This hole wasn't just any hole. It was to be six feet deep. Richard, being a kind one and all, assisted me. When we were five feet down, dad got home, had a conniption and declared it to be—too deep! Around five hours later, and three and a half feet of dirt refilled, I finally put the tree in, all of its foot and half of roots."

Dave had to get up early in order to seize the day for himself. One Saturday morning, he and Rich rose at 6:30 a.m. and hopped on their bikes. They had "a whole lot of fun riding on the nature trails, climbing, and lying on picnic tables." Dave called it "the most enjoyable bike hike ever." Dave's desire to grab the day before it grasped him didn't always work out; activities seemed to steamroll his time. He eventually learned to carve time out each day, if only to execute his daily jogs.

Friends talk of "classic Dave" moments—situations that exemplified his personality. One example was illustrated in his diary; he was still a sophomore. Dave's sandy blond hair with its signature quarter-size dark patch on the back of his head, his clear blue eyes, ready smile, and slender frame made for a nice-looking young man. But despite his good looks, sweet disposition, and sense of humor, when a girl asked him to the Turnabout Dance, he was shocked and wrote, "I thought she hated me." Then he agonized over what to do next—*Do I buy the tickets or will she?* In classic Dave fashion, he went out of his way to stroll past the girl's house on two occasions hoping to bump into her, which would negate the need to make what he felt would be an awkward phone call. His innovative idea did not pay off, and he wrote, "Someday maybe that tactful action will be successful."

Dave eventually made the call and was so nervous when he dialed the girl's number that he rushed inside a closet and closed the door so he couldn't hang up. He wrote, "I felt like an idiot. . . . I couldn't think of what to say." After the dance, insecurity caused him to wonder if the girl had had a good time with him as her date.

Another classic Dave trait showed up in his diary. In the back are pages with a cash account for each month; there he recorded every dime he earned or spent. Among entries such as ice cream, film, and a dog collar, are gems of generosity— he spent considerable amounts on gifts for his mom, dad, and sister. His sense of personal responsibility was apparent when he bought his own shoes, socks, and suspenders; he wrote, "I can afford it; besides, it would probably be inconvenient for mom or dad."

Unassuming. Humble. Indirect. These traits made Dave who he was. A respectful, thoughtful, sometimes painfully shy guy.

Dave was also known for his sense of commitment, but sometimes this was a double-edged sword that interfered with control over his time. When he was asked to attend a weeklong Boy Scout leadership camp after he'd already devoted six weeks of his vacation to summer school, he said yes even though he craved free time during the few remaining summer days. Dave often said yes when he meant no. When a scoutmaster asked him to join the gun club, Dave wrote in his diary, "I don't want to, but I will anyway."

Dave's struggle over how to spend his time was ongoing. On a summer day he wrote, "I feel as if today was wasted even though I didn't lay idle." He took pictures of kids at a local park, then developed and printed the pictures in the darkroom of his home. This was a good day's work as a budding photographer; however, he'd wanted to see his friends that day. Then when he played tennis with a friend, he lamented that he should have cleaned his room, the den, and the downstairs bathroom. (These were his assigned chores.)

Dave clearly wanted to accomplish much more than he had time for, but what's striking is the sheer volume of activities contained in one year. He struggled in some subjects but did well in school overall. He attended summer school to squeeze in an extra class, he devoted endless hours to scouting activities, and he began a career as a photographer. Also, he was First Chair clarinet in the school concert band, he was in Marching Band, he learned German, and he tended to chores such as cleaning, cooking, and caring for the family pet. Despite this long list, he berated himself for not achieving more.

41

As Dave neared his sixteenth birthday, the pressure of keeping up with his studies and too many other demands on his time caught up with him. On December 1, he wrote, "One could say that today is the beginning of the end. The first day of the last month of 1965, when I lived most of my sixteenth year of existence . . . I am in trouble now as far as grades go. . . . The problem is algebra. I can't remember anything, which is due to two factors. Number 1, I don't pay much attention in class. Number 2, I never study at all." Algebra builds on previously learned concepts; once he fell behind, catching up would have felt impossible.

Too many commitments were like extra layers of clothing that weighed Dave down, and he began to shed what he could. He quit scouts. His goal of filling up every line of his diary disappeared. Perhaps he didn't want to record thoughts that reached a new level of maturity. He mentioned a girl. He wrote that his father was angry about something. Whatever the case, he left most of the pages in December blank. He turned sixteen on December 18; he had written on that page two months earlier to wish himself a happy birthday. His last entry for the year was on December 19—a few words of anger. His age certainly figured into negativity he felt at that time. Anger is always a secondary emotion; so what came first? Feelings of frustration? Weariness? Anxiety? Likely all three.

Again, every generation has its challenges but the 1960s seemed to spew coming-of-age struggles.

President John F. Kennedy was assassinated in 1963; Dave recalled the event in his diary: "When we heard on the radio that our President was dead, I broke down in tears and I tried to make myself believe I was dreaming."

Dave was an aware teenager who watched President Lyndon B. Johnson's speech about civil rights after the 1965 march in Selma, Alabama, resulted in savagery. All these images, including nonstop Vietnam War coverage, were brought into America's living rooms like never before. It was enough to agitate even the calmest of souls.

Dave worried about his family's safety. When his parents went on a weekend trip, he fretted about the drive and felt a rush of relief when they returned. His worries were reinforced by repeated reminders that young lives can and do get snuffed out. A boy from his baseball league was struck and killed while walking to the field; Dave's father was president of the baseball association at the time and the whole family was shaken. That the game had been canceled due to rain compounded the grief.

Dave also wrote in his diary about a boy who snuck into a friend's swimming pool and drowned: "The fireman who dragged him out realized it was his own son!" Also, Dave's job as a freelance newspaper photographer drew tragedy into his viewfinder. When his sister witnessed a car accident, fifteen-year-old Dave said, "I grabbed my camera and within five minutes, I was taking pictures. It was an awful accident! A man went through the windshield."

Growing up close to death in his home and community, with sonic booms overhead, nuclear fallout shelters across America, and news of almost two thousand Americans killed in Vietnam in 1965 alone (a number that more than quadrupled the following year)—all these were shadows that passed over Dave Johnston's youth—stumbling blocks on the path to adulthood. Understandably, he considered his own early demise. He once said to his parents, "Just bury me in a pine box." He didn't mean to be macabre. He just didn't want the fanfare. Also, it was a statement borne out of respect and love for the earth; he didn't want to be placed inside a fiberglass capsule to take up a piece of real estate for evermore.

Dave's 1965 diary was a microcosm of the man he became. It contains many moments that tug at the heart, such as when he wrote, "The unusual event for my entire life was that I shaved away hair that took me more than fifteen and a half years to accumulate. Maybe I should have buried it. Well, no worry, when I'm thirty-one years old, I'll have more." But he wouldn't reach thirty-one.

The following year, 1966, saw sixteen-year-old Dave enter his senior year of high school, where he discovered cross-country running—an activity that would have a big impact on his physique, stamina, and anxiety level.

The end of his senior year was capped with the deadly tornado in his hometown—as though the earth heard his ponderings about the possibility of an early death.

IT'S EASY TO STAND IN THE CROWD BUT IT
TAKES COURAGE TO STAND ALONE.

Mahatma Gandhi

PART TWO

COMING OF AGE

CURIOSITY IS A GIFT, A CAPACITY FOR
PLEASURE IN KNOWING.

John Ruskin

COLLEGE YEARS AND
SHIFTING GEARS

Dave's senior picture. Used with permission of Johnston family and Harold L. Richards High School.

MERE WEEKS AFTER THE OAK LAWN TORNADO, the dead had been buried, rebuilding efforts had begun, and Dave Johnston graduated high school.

As the band played the graduation march for Dave and his classmates at Harold L. Richards High School, background music blared from the other side of the globe in the form of ferocious fighting in Vietnam. The graduation stage and the world stage seemed at opposite ends of the spectrum, except that they weren't. At almost the exact time that Dave graduated from Richards, the "Nine Days in May Border Battles" raged and reminded graduating seniors that with each step, they marched toward an uncertain future. An eighteen-year-old soldier spoke about the battles that began May 18, 1967: "At the end of the day, I was amazed I had survived, and it had just begun." A medic described enemy fire that slammed into their position "like rainfall."[1] When the Nine Days battles ended, posthumous Medals of Honor were awarded.

Troop buildup more than tripled from 1965 to 1966; and from 1965 to 1967, it had increased more than fivefold.[2] Young American men were exiting high school graduation stages and entering the Vietnam stage of operations. But Dave's December birthday meant he was still seventeen when he left for college in fall 1967.

By April 1968, near the end of Dave's freshman year of college, American troop strength in Vietnam reached its peak—over half a million soldiers were on the ground. About one in ten young American men served in Vietnam, including two of Dave's childhood friends—John Baird and Kenneth Gooley entered the service. Both their exits would be blocked by death. John and Ken (or Kent as he liked to be called in high school) grew up on the same block with Dave. They joined scouts together and played baseball at the local park. Both friends showed up in Dave's teenage diary, but history added its own pages.

Dave was a band kid all through high school. The only sports he joined were tennis during his junior year and cross country during his senior year. Running was the sport that best suited him because his small size wasn't necessarily a liability. He was able to run as part of a team.

Dave embraced running for many reasons. He had worked out for years, hoping to increase muscle strength, and running did this. It is also possible that he saw running as a way to prepare for service in Vietnam. With troop strength ever-increasing, war service seemed inevitable. If one considers oneself weaker or less physically capable, the thought of survival of the fittest could be a spur to action.

Running afforded Dave time away from prying eyes, alone time that he treasured. It cleared his head; the world melted away for a while. But he wasn't running away from anything. On the contrary, running carried him into the future. It built his endurance for a career that would be physically demanding. It also turned into a routine that gave him the semblance of control in what felt like an uncontrollable world. Later, running brought him together with people who would figure large in his life, both personally and professionally.

So it was that in fall 1967, Dave left home with a suitcase and his running shoes and became the first in his family to attend college. He chose the University of

Dave on cross-country team. Used with permission of
Johnston family and Harold L. Richards High School.

Illinois because of its reputation and for financial reasons—as a state school it
was affordable. He also chose the school for its proximity to Oak Lawn—just
two hours due south. The school is situated in the middle of the state latitudi-
nally, with farmland hugging its perimeters—a bucolic setting for a guy from
the suburbs of Chicago.

Dave had saved his money. He also worked summers while at the University
of Illinois as an Oak Lawn postman to help pay college expenses. The work was

mostly outdoors and he got a kick out of reading residents' unusual names. His favorite was Patsy Patti—the first and last names of which were nicknames for his sister.

At first, photojournalism seemed a logical degree for Dave to pursue. He had worked as a photographer since he was fifteen. He'd even won an award from the University of Iowa for a photo he took at a local baseball game. The journalism path unfolded in front of him, one supported by his parents, and he set his feet upon it. However, like tectonic plates, something inside him shifted when he took a geology class. Two plates converged and journalism was subducted. Dave switched his degree focus and set about becoming a geologist.

The shift fit Dave's likes and dislikes.

He liked being outdoors. Some of what made school miserable for him growing up was that feeling of being stuck—he once compared having a day off from high school as "being let out of prison." Earth science had beckoned Dave since boyhood when he amassed his first rock collection and spent many hours labeling them. Once when he got hold of a moon rock, he showed childhood chum Bob Swedko, who said Dave "glowed" when he showed it off. Bob was less impressed: "It's a rock, man." But Dave couldn't help himself. To him, it was a mystery that begged to be solved. What forces combined to produce it? How do moon rocks differ from those formed on Earth? And how, if at all, are they similar?

Not only did Dave dislike being trapped indoors, he abhorred treading into spaces where he didn't feel welcome. Award-winning photographer Mark Cohen said that many fear "street photography" because it invades the subject's personal space.[3] Dave wrote in his diary, "I took pictures for the newspaper of kids at the park, ages two to fifteen. I felt dumb and very conspicuous." Also, Dave hated messing up shots—he berated himself every time he failed to center his subject or execute an excellent photograph.

Family folklore has it that Dave got a bad grade at the University of Illinois and this was the impetus for his selection of a geology class. Pat recalls that math tripped him up, but another family member said it was English. Tom Johnston had said Dave merely took the class as an elective, a choice every college student makes. Whatever it was, Dave's first geology class proved to be a turning point. His lifelong love of science sparked something inside him and he seized the opportunity to forge a new path.

In a way, Dave was on track for both science and writing. Except that journalists document the news, and many geologists make the news with their findings.

When Dave entered college, volcanology was poised to reach a new level of understanding and gain recognition for its importance worldwide. This was due in large part to the modern theory of plate tectonics that had taken hold in the late 1960s.

Since 1915, German meteorologist Alfred Wegener's proposal that Earth's continents had once been connected was unproven. Wegener theorized that a supercontinent broke apart due to what he called continental displacement. However, his theory was rejected by geologists. Then the Cold War ushered in the Nuclear Test-Ban Treaty of 1963, which prohibited the testing of nuclear weapons in the atmosphere or underwater. To ensure compliance by countries that might ignore the ban, a global network of sensors was installed that could detect any nuclear testing around the world; the sensors also picked up on earthquakes. Scientists soon realized that earthquakes and volcanic activity occur almost exclusively at the edges of seven major tectonic plates and dozens of smaller minor plates and microplates that make up the earth's crust.[4] As these plates bump into, pull away from, or sideswipe each other, they transform the earth's surface. Mountains or rifts are formed, and earthquakes are triggered. Wegener's idea is now accepted as the theory of continental drift.

The Juan de Fuca microplate is wedged between the North American and Pacific plates and is largely responsible for the mountains in America's Pacific Northwest—the Cascade Range, which includes Mount St. Helens.

Perhaps it was Dave's minerology course that solidified his love for geology. For it was this class that took him to a temple of stacked lava flows in Michigan's Upper Peninsula (UP), where there were once active volcanoes. The area on the UP's Keweenaw Peninsula contains one of the largest exposed lava flows on earth. Called "Copper Country," it also contains one of the largest copper deposits in the world. According to the Keweenaw National Park, "At over 1,640 feet thick, the 'greenstone flow' would have existed as a magma sea for hundreds if not a thousand years when it was deposited. . . . It would have been an impressive and terrible sight." And that's just *one* of a series of lava flows in the area. Deposited a billion years ago, these layers were thrust upward by the Keweenaw fault, which bisects the peninsula, so that the layers are nearer to the surface

Dave's first University of Illinois field trip. Photo courtesy of Chris Carlson.

where humans can see them. It is there that Dave collected his first lava and rhyolite and experienced the roots of his first volcano.

During four years at college, Dave traveled twenty-seven thousand miles to see exposed geology. One could say that the field trips were a kind of extreme sport. Dave and his classmates attended a summer field camp in Sheridan, Wyoming, and worked in one hundred–degree heat. They clamored around the Bighorn Mountains all day and drafted maps half the night. Dave's friend and field partner Joe Jakupcak said, "To relax, two guys across the hall lined an entire wall of their room with empty Coors cans." And Dave? "He relaxed by running," said Joe. "Not really jogging—but flat-out running a few miles every day. I sat on a fire escape, dead tired, and watched Dave lope off across the hills into the haze until he was out of sight."

Along with growth spurts during Dave's early years at college, which added several inches to his frame (topping out at just under six feet), the daily workouts and running he started in high school contributed to an ever-increasing stamina. Dave's friend from his cross-country high school days, Bob Swedko, said, "Dave and I were pretty disgusting when we started but we got better." Dave eventually got so much better that weekly twenty-mile runs became part of his routine—runs he completed with a fellow geologist and friend during their downtime. This helped him to scale four thousand vertical feet for days in a row during geological fieldwork.

Running during downtime was Dave's thing. When he found himself back in Oak Lawn for a holiday, he called his old buddy Bob to go running. Both men went to Illinois state schools, and both found themselves home one cold Thanksgiving weekend. The two planned to meet up, and Bob arrived at Dave's house to find him decked out in pink tights under his running shorts; he was ready to go. (Had Dave asked Pat to borrow her tights? Perhaps he had to sign a contract!) Bob had long johns under his shorts, and away they went down Ninety-Fifth Street. It wasn't long before Dave's pink tights attracted the attention of a group of teenage boys in a car. While running down a busy thoroughfare, Dave and Bob found the same car blocking their path at the cross-streets. After the fourth time of running around the vehicle, Dave leaped on top of their harassers' car, up and over he went, and kept on running. Two of the boys jumped from the car in hot pursuit, while the others drove to the next intersecting street. "You go that way! See you back at your parents' house!" The two men split up and sprinted away from their pursuers.

College campuses across America seemed under siege in the 1960s—from war protests that turned bloody to demands for racial and gender equality that resulted in arrests. Dave met someone directly involved in advancing the rights of black Americans—an encounter he considered an honor, which came about because of Dave's habit of running at every opportunity.

Thanks to Dave's friend Bob, former Olympian Oscar Moore had a walk-on (or run-on) role in Dave's life. Both Bob and Moore were on the track team at Southern Illinois University, and when Bob told Dave about the star at his school, Dave was awestruck. So next time Dave visited Bob at school, there was a surprise in store—Bob arranged for the three of them to run together.

Moore, who began running to alleviate anxiety, was one of many pioneers who advanced the civil rights movement when he participated in the 1964 Olympics. Moore described how much black Olympians sacrificed; he lost his job when he made the team. Moore was injured and couldn't compete in the 1968 Olympics, which occurred six months after Martin Luther King Jr. was assassinated. In a historic moment aimed at advancing awareness of the civil rights movement, two black track stars who medaled in 1968, Tommie Smith and John Carlos, raised their black-gloved fists high in the air while America's anthem was played.[5] Moore's cousin ran in the 1968 Olympics; he chose to wear black socks to signal solidarity.

When Dave arrived on the University of Illinois's campus in 1967, only 1 percent of its students were black.[6] After King's assassination, the university started a program to increase enrollment of underrepresented students. Lack of scholarship funds and housing presented challenges to the new program and more protests ensued. The Black Students Association was formed at the University of Illinois, and a list of demands was submitted to the university's administration in 1969; the list was a catalyst for considerable changes at the campus.

College not only raises civic consciousness but also transforms people in other ways. For Dave, it was during his time at the University of Illinois that he began to feel more confident around women. He met his first girlfriend and fell hard.

They spoke of marriage. However, the relationship didn't work out, largely because they differed in their religious views. Dave read the Bible and discarded its estimation that the earth is between six thousand and fifteen thousand years old.[7]

It was also during Dave's college days that he befriended someone who would ultimately change his life—Doug Lalla. Doug shared Dave's passions for science and running, and he would later influence Dave's PhD research, which in turn impacted his career path. The two men met as members of the University of Illinois's track team and shared practice runs among cornfields. Doug remembers that Dave always did more than was expected—he did speed work after every workout. Doug said, "Dave pushed himself so hard, he'd throw up." In a study on adversity and resilience, psychologist Meg Jay found a man who, like Dave, had also been the youngest and smallest among his peers and grew up feeling socially vulnerable. This man, called "Paul" in Jay's study, started running as a teen and designed workouts that increasingly pushed his limits. As an adult, Paul continued relentless physical training because, in his words, "I worried I'd relapse and end up like I used to be."[8]

In high school, the cross-country team Dave belonged to was called "one of the worst." Those days were behind him; but they continued to push him.

Dave and Doug formed a close friendship, and years later a phone call from Doug would take Dave to the doorstep of his first active volcano. But first they had to get through college.

In December 1969, the Vietnam War Draft Board instituted a lottery to determine the order in which men would be called for induction into the military during 1970. The 1969 lottery applied to all men born between January 1, 1944, and December 31, 1950, including Dave and Doug. Three hundred sixty-six blue plastic capsules were placed in a glass container; each contained a birth date during the calendar year. With television cameras rolling, capsules were hand-pulled one at a time; the order in which they were drawn determined the "order-of-call" for men ages eighteen to twenty-six years old. The first birth date drawn was September 14 and assigned draft number 001. Thus, all men born on September 14 in the years 1944 to 1950 were assigned 001. The remaining blue capsules were drawn, and the order in which they were pulled was the number assigned to each date. Dave's birth date, December 18, was in the capsule drawn on the 128th pull; thus, he was assigned draft number 128.

In 1970, the Selective Service called up men assigned draft numbers 001 through 195. Dave's number fell within this group; however, only those who would finish their undergrad degree during 1970 were required to report for duty. (Automatic draft deferments applied to men pursuing undergrad degrees who would *not* finish in the year called.) Dave was only a junior in college at the time; he received another deferment.

However, Dave's friend Doug was a college senior; he would finish his bachelor's in spring 1970, and his number fell within the range of 001 to 195. Doug was directed to report for service in summer 1970, and like many others, he filed an appeal. The appeal process wasn't finished when it came time to sign up for the fall semester at the University of Illinois, so Doug registered. He later lost the appeal, but he was allowed to finish the school year and graduated with his master's in physics in spring 1971. A few weeks later, he was inducted into the army.

As Doug prepared to report to boot camp, Dave graduated from the University of Illinois in spring 1971 with "Highest Honors and Distinction in Geology."

The kind of job Dave dreamed of required a doctorate in geology, which required four more years of schooling. That is, it would have taken him an extra four years if he hadn't changed paths again, which he did. At a point when he was almost at the writing stage for his PhD on the project he originally chose, he switched from the study of one volcano to another. It took Dave seven years to achieve his doctorate. In total, he spent eleven years at two universities.

When Dave enrolled in graduate school at the University of Washington in Seattle, more Americans were pursuing advanced education than ever before. The rate of doctorates conferred in the United States increased steadily between the mid-1960s and mid-1970s.[*] Since American troop strength in Vietnam declined starting in 1971, it seemed Dave would be able to complete his graduate work without being called for service. (Troop numbers dropped from 334,000 in 1970 to just under 157,000 in 1971; then down to 24,000 in 1972; the United States withdrew combat troops in March 1973.)

Seattle was half a continent away from Oak Lawn. Even so, Dave's parents supported his choice. Nestled in the Pacific Northwest, the University of Washington's earth science program is among the best.

---

[*] Doctorates conferred increased at an average rate of 10 percent per year, according to Cornell Higher Education Research Institute.

Dave tried not to overburden his parents financially, but when he switched his PhD focus this created some tension at home. One friend remembered that when Dave ran low on money, he bought bushels of potatoes to get by for weeks at a time. Dave also borrowed money rather than ask his parents. Pat loaned him all she had at the time, and Doug loaned him a sizable amount. (It took years but Dave paid both back.)

It was the summer between the University of Illinois and the University of Washington—1971—and Dave needed a job. Luckily, one of Dave's undergraduate professors recognized him as a "bright graduate" and recommended him to Peter Lipman, who needed a summer field assistant. Pete was a well-respected volcanologist with the U.S. Geological Survey (USGS) who worked in the San Juan Mountains volcanic field of southwestern Colorado—some of its peaks reached the highest altitudes of the western United States. Pete hired Dave, and Pete became Dave's mentor and friend. Much later, they would become USGS colleagues and work together at Mount St. Helens in 1980.

Together, Pete and Dave sampled volcanic rocks 25 to 35 million years old. From this work, a picture emerged of how the mountains, or volcanoes, had grown. On a typical day, the two men went up and down ridges, identifying rocks as they went; climbing three thousand to five thousand vertical feet each day. Once they identified the by-products of a volcano, they created a map of the geological formations that made up the area.

It was very complicated terrain, but Dave caught on quickly and Pete rehired him the next summer. Dave had learned so much the previous year that they were able to split up and cover a very large area. Dave and Pete had two "amazing" summers together, according to Pete. However, Dave had a "problem" that needed to be addressed—it seemed he didn't want to stop at the end of the workday. "I had to order Dave to come in at night so we could get an early start the next morning," said Pete.

Dave had another problem—he had never driven a manual stick shift. Also, as an Illinois boy, he'd never driven in hilly country, his home state being predominantly flat. Pete said, "Driving the stick shift was harder for Dave to understand than rocks. Finally, I gave him the keys and told him to go practice." Pete's nerves could take a lot but Dave's driving proved too much.

During those two summers with Pete and his family, Dave fell in love again—not just with the people who came to look upon him as family, but with a vision for the future. Professionally and personally, Dave thought Pete's life was perfect. He camped with his family during summers—slept in tents and used a camper for a kitchen and office. Dave told his parents, "I want a job like Pete's! And I want a wife and kids like Pete's!" Pete mirrored the admiration: "Dave was special. . . . I thought of him as a third son."[9] Dave was intent on achieving the perfect life, as modeled by his mentor.

Before Dave finished that second summer in Colorado, Pete gave him "permission" to use a new title. Dave wrote to his parents and said that Pete no longer thought of him as a field assistant. Dave wrote, "I am now a full-fledged geologist." In that letter, he described a rare physical feature he didn't know he had; he said his growing mustache "shows up better because it is turning red from the sun." This combination of blond hair and red mustache or beard isn't from the sun; it results from inheritance of a mutated version of the MC1R gene (those with two unmutated copies have red hair on head *and* face). He also said he was getting "dark," and joked that it was due to . . . soil: "I bathe in a stream fed by melting snow and seepage from valley bottoms. If you bathed in water that cold, twice a week would seem like a lot to you too!" Then he closed the letter by signing—for the first time in his life—"David A. Johnston, Geologist."

In summer 1973, Dave returned to the San Juan Mountains to conduct his own research. For his PhD thesis, he chose to map, date, and conduct a geochemical study of the extinct Cimarron Volcano, part of the San Juan complex. Dave had written a proposal and was granted a stipend of eight hundred dollars from the University of Washington. Dave needed to stretch the money to include a field assistant. He wanted Doug Lalla, whose military service was almost at an end. A peace agreement had been signed by North Vietnam, South Vietnam, and the United States in January, and American combat troops were withdrawn in March. There was a rule at the time that anyone with a job waiting could get out of the military thirty days early. So Dave wrote a letter to the army, and Doug's discharge date was moved up to May 19, 1973—in time to help Dave with the Cimarron fieldwork.

Dave wrote a post card to his family with a return address of: "D. Johnston, General Delivery, Montrose, Colorado 80401." He said that he and Doug were having "a really groovy time" and that he'd had to buy thirty dollars worth of "extra safety" by buying an ice ax. The money from the stipend didn't stretch far.

They had to use Doug's truck to get into the mountains. For food, they chose a cheap protein source—Loma Linda soy burgers. They also enjoyed any cookies that arrived via general delivery. Dave was famous for eating more than his share of cookies while in the field, for which he felt guilty, but it didn't stop him.

Like ants on their hill, Dave and Doug swarmed the area. There were countless drainages, and they had to climb up each one. "I was more of a mule for Dave," said Doug. "I was a physicist, not a rock guy."

Ravines dissect the volcano at different spots and are different ages. Dave needed samples from *all* ravines; only then could he get an idea of the composition and the big picture of the volcano. The highest drainage had a steep overhang and no way to get up without climbing the precipitous face. Dave was determined. So he set aside his fear, held onto the embedded rocks that jutted out, and ascended. When he got to the top, he puked. In order to be thorough, he paid a queasy price, but he got the samples he needed.

It was during the regular school semesters at the University of Washington that Dave became aware of another geology student—Christine Carlson. Like Dave, Chris started out studying a different field in college, took a geology class, fell in love with it, and switched her major. She remembers the day a professor referred to the beautiful snowy Cascade Mountains as volcanoes that could still be active. He said there was a chance of an eruption in the Cascades in the students' lifetime; Chris went home that day wondering which one it might be.

As it happened, Dave was *very* aware of Chris. But rather than approach her, he took the path most comfortable for him. "Dave asked someone where I lived," said Chris, "and then changed his running route to the block where he thought he'd pass me, but it was the wrong block! After we dated a while, he told how he spent so much time running up and down that block hoping to run into me on the way to school; this was classic Dave." By this Chris meant that Dave was very creative—"Once he thought he knew where I lived, it would be just like him to put a plan into place."

What Chris couldn't know is that Dave employed this tactic of passing by a girl's house when he was in high school. It was his unassuming way of handling the situation—he didn't presume that Chris would be interested in him or welcome his advances. While his ploy didn't work in high school or in college—the females did *not* come out of their homes at opportune times—things worked out. Dave went to that high school dance and he eventually entered into a relationship with Chris.

After Doug Lalla's stint with Dave the summer of 1973, he moved on to the University of Alaska Fairbanks (UAF), and he and Dave remained close friends. When Dave found himself with fieldwork in Alaska during the summer Doug was to be married, Doug asked Dave to be his best man. But the timing didn't unfold as planned. "Dave was busy gathering gas-sampling gear," said Doug. The bride's brother stepped in as best man and the justice of the peace presided. "Dave showed up the next day; we hung out and barbequed burgers. It was all good," said Doug.

Other friends saw Dave's occasional challenges in planning out his time. They said he wasn't inconsiderate—he was "optimistic when estimating timelines"— he thought he could wrap things up quicker than he could.

Dave's research took him to the Azores Islands off mainland Portugal and to some of the highest peaks in western America. He worked at Mount Katmai and Novarupta in the Valley of Ten Thousand Smokes in Alaska. But it was Mount St. Augustine that changed his life.

In summer 1975, Dave was about at the writing stage for his PhD on Cimarron Volcano when Doug called. Doug had funding for a summer graduate project and needed a field assistant. Would Dave like to be Doug's assistant at Alaska's Mount St. Augustine? "To work on a real volcano, not one of those dead ones," as Doug put it. Dave seized the opportunity. Doug had obtained a grant from the Department of Energy to conduct a thermal survey of the volcano; his project was one of many that took place as part of the UAF's Geophysical Institute's survey of Augustine. The Geophysical Institute assembled a team of scientists, including Doug and Dave, and they all spent thirty days at Augustine that summer.

Mount St. Augustine is on an uninhabited island made up entirely of deposits of the volcano. Located in lower Cook Inlet, Augustine is the most active volcano of the eastern Aleutian arc. It is a stratovolcano—the most picturesque and deadly of all volcano types. Over the past two thousand years, Augustine has erupted often, and at least eleven of its large debris avalanches reached the sea.

Its largest historical eruption was in 1883; a debris avalanche caused a tsunami that sent sixty-two-foot waves across the sea and hit coastal areas seventy miles away.[10] Other major eruptions occurred in 1935 and 1963–64. Due to Augustine's frequent activity and hazardous nature, a network of seismometers was installed in 1971.

Mere months after the team of scientists conducted their geophysical survey of Augustine in summer 1975, a new eruptive phase began in January 1976—one that almost took the lives of Dave and Doug.

On January 22, 1976, Augustine erupted explosively, which jostled the seismometers that had been installed there. Seismometers were a window into what was happening in the area, and with some of the machinery disabled, scientists couldn't record important data. After a brief period of quietude from Augustine, the Geophysical Institute dispatched a team to fix the sensors, including Doug and Dave. On the February day they chose to go, the skies looked threatening. The pilot thought a storm was brewing and was hesitant, but the team's leader was persuasive; money changed hands and the helicopter took off for Augustine Island.

Once they landed at Augustine, ash blew and a storm moved out of Cook Inlet toward the men. The helicopter pilot realized take-off would be impossible; he needed to alert his superiors with the transportation company. It was hard to get a radio signal while on the ground, so the pilot took the helicopter up just high enough to be able to transmit a message. The chopper lifted a few hundred feet, then it was blown back down to the beach. The pilot was shaken but fine; however, the chopper sustained significant damage. This meant no one could go anywhere, even once the storm lifted. Thus began three long days, stuck on an island with an active volcano and a blinding blizzard. The mission of repairing sensors was scrapped in favor of *survival*.

"We shouldn't have gone," said Doug.

The men took refuge in a shack that was built years earlier when seismometers were first installed. Made of corrugated steel, the shack had four walls, a roof with holes created by hot rocks that erupted from the volcano during multiple eruptions on January 22–25, a triple bunk bed with the middle bunk incinerated by the heat from the window it sat next to—and there was . . . no heat. The tools at the men's disposal consisted of a disabled helicopter, some jet fuel, and

61

innovation. They constructed a heat source from a tank, generator, tube, and rock. They tried to vent the gases out of the shack but awoke the first night to a black layer of smoke hovering above them. Asphyxiation was added to the list of dangers that threatened their lives.

When the weather cleared on the third day, their only means of rescue arrived—a chopper. Its pilot came bearing two-day-old doughnuts. The transport company felt so bad about the ordeal that they agreed to fly the men all the way to Fairbanks (420 miles versus the 100-mile hop back to the airport the men departed from three days earlier). About the time Dave and Doug returned to Fairbanks, a report hit the newswire—"Volcanologists Escape with Their Lives." Augustine erupted less than twelve hours after the team's escape, in the early hours of February 6.

Dave originally was going to do both his master's and PhD on the extinct Cimarron Volcano. But after his visit to Augustine in summer 1975, he asked his thesis advisor if he could switch his PhD thesis from Cimarron to Augustine. Dave saw research into the role gas plays in an eruption as an opportunity to better understand a volcano's pre-eruptive activity. This advancement in understanding could in turn mitigate risk and save lives—perhaps then no one would fly to a volcanic island where an eruption was imminent. Dave's adviser told him to finish Cimarron first, because at the time the University of Washington required doctoral students to complete a master's degree before continuing on to a PhD.

However, when Augustine erupted in 1976, this meant Dave's research from 1975 was from *before* the eruption. Dave wanted to compare before and after samples. Time was ticking. His thesis committee gave him the green light to switch his PhD to Augustine with the caveat that he still needed to write up his Cimarron project. Dave jumped at the chance and immediately immersed himself in Augustine.

Switching his PhD focus to Augustine felt like starting over since Dave's work on Cimarron was basically complete, except for the writing. The shift was a big deal because he went from historical geology, which is the study of the earth's formations over time, including inactive volcanoes such as Cimarron, to physical geology, which focuses on the processes that form the earth's features, including active volcanoes such as Augustine. Still, Dave went for it. He shunted Cimarron into a master's, and twenty-five months later he defended two theses; one on Cimarron and the other on Augustine. This is how it came to be that Dave completed pretty much the equivalent of *two* PhDs.[11]

After the January and February 1976 eruptions, Augustine erupted sporadically between April 6 and April 23, then it settled down; all was quiet.[12] Dave planned his return to Augustine that summer to study its evolving dome and changing gas chemistry. With renewed funding, Dave as head of the project selected a field assistant—again he asked Doug. The plan was for the two men to be dropped off for thirty days. Having barely escaped death there, Dave wrote to his sister before he left for the field and expressed trepidation; he didn't want to get "fried."

Once they were back at Augustine, Dave and Doug found that the new dome sloughed off rock material from the summit—small and large chunks tumbled down the sides of the mountain toward them. They also found that the side with the most amount of rockfall was the easiest route to the summit—dubbed the "gates of hell," it was a dangerous path but it was the quickest. So the two scientists passed through the "gates." Once they safely reached the summit crater, they were rewarded with their choice of fumaroles (volcanic vents that emit hot gases) to use for their work.

The men set up their camp near the summit and conducted daily experiments. Camping at the summit saved traipsing up and down Augustine's flanks. It also meant they could use the volcano's fumaroles as stoves to cook their food; however, the fumaroles demanded respect. One day as Dave started to take a sample from one, the mountain breathed and hot steam exuded from the vent and singed the hair off his arm. "It could have killed him," said Doug.

Indeed, it seemed that Augustine had a vendetta to settle, and Dave and Doug were in its crosshairs. A brutal storm brewed once again. A strong wind lifted their tent with them inside and stuff banged against their heads. When the storm let up a bit, their camp was in shambles and they had to get down the mountain.

Icy sleet and rain made their descent treacherous. At one point, Doug slid hundreds of feet and had to use his ice ax to save himself from hitting a boulder. They were able to reach the Geophysical Institute's corrugated shack—the one with plastic that melted and drooped as a reminder of the high heat Augustine produced earlier that year—temperatures that would have killed them if they hadn't escaped in time. Dave and Doug used the shack for the last week of their thirty-day fieldwork rather than attempt to reestablish camp at the mountain's summit. Food supplies ran low during that last week—a constant problem in the field—canned peaches sustained them until their scheduled ride showed up.

The following summer, in 1977, was Dave's last required research trip to complete his PhD. Again, he planned a thirty-day excursion to Alaska. Doug Lalla was busy with wedding plans so Dave asked Lee Fairchild to be his field assistant. Lee was a classmate from the University of Washington whose enthusiasm for volcanology matched Dave's. To sample Augustine's fumaroles, the men climbed four thousand feet to the summit crater. Once inside the crater, Dave and Lee found it was too hot to stand for more than about thirty seconds; their boots would have melted after about a minute. So they stood off to the side, cooled off, then ran into the crater over and over to collect samples. One day, Dave stuck a thermometer inside a fumarole and it shot up to 300 degrees Celsius (570 degrees Fahrenheit). The two men didn't know if it was hot rock or magma, so they ran down the volcano, and at the bottom they couldn't help laughing at themselves. They reasoned that since Augustine hadn't erupted for over a year, it was unlikely that magma had caused the thermometer's rise. Also, they were only halfway through their thirty-day stint and there was a lot of work left to do. So they went to the shack, found a solid iron bar, and took it back to the fumarole. They figured, "If it clinks, it's rock; if it's magma we'll have a sample." Dave doubled up on protective gloves, inserted the rod in the fumarole and heard, "Clink!" The men were relieved; until Dave's gloves began to smolder and he threw the iron bar, which sailed through the air like a limp noodle. After the hot rock drama, they collected all the samples they needed.

In retrospect, returning to that fumarole sounds too risky; however, Lee explained their decision: "We felt it was a reasonable calculated risk; and given the same situation, I'd do it again."[13]

In addition to Augustine, other volcanoes in the area garnered Dave's attention. He performed work that summer at Redoubt and Iliamna volcanoes. With the help of a U.S. Army Chinook helicopter, he found himself on the summit of all three within the space of ten days. The army, as it happened, was eager to help geologists because they thought their participation might lead to discovery of an army airplane that crashed on Iliamna the previous February. But Iliamna's snow accumulation was twenty feet (after snowmelt), which made discovery of the airplane impossible. (According to Dave's notes, it was the second army airplane that had been lost on Iliamna.)

In a letter to his parents to let them know he was "safely off the volcano," Dave talked of "exciting features" he found on the summit of Redoubt—"evidence of a phreatomagmatic explosion." He planned to write a proposal to the National Science Foundation to fund work there.

Dave saw a future in Alaska, but first he had to defend his PhD dissertation. He wasn't looking forward to standing and talking in front of his thesis committee—a daunting task for someone afraid of public speaking.

DAVE WIGGLED LIKE JELL-O, THEN DROPPED.

Chris Carlson

5

STAGE FRIGHT

THE AUDITORIUM WAS HUGE AND IT WAS PACKED. It seemed the entire volcanology community had come to the 1977 Geological Society of America (GSA) meeting to hear about Mount St. Augustine's eruption.

Dave was slated to speak about his work there. He thought he would copresent with Hans Ulrich-Schmincke, a volcanologist and visiting scientist at USGS–Menlo Park who also had conducted research at Augustine. Dave and Hans had prepared a joint abstract for the meeting, but at the last minute Dave found he would be presenting alone. A senior geologist handed Dave some slides and said, "You can do this." He was unprepared; his nervousness skyrocketed.

Dave started the presentation and seemed to be doing okay until . . . wham. He disappeared from behind the podium. The panel chair rushed to the microphone and asked, "Is there a doctor in the house?" Even though every person in the audience was a PhD, no one could do anything. Then as quickly as he'd disappeared, Dave popped back up, stood at the podium, and started talking again.

Then two slides later . . . down he went again. When he came to, Dave was surprised and annoyed with himself and asked, "Oh shit, did I do that again?"

After the second faint, the panel chairperson moved Dave over to sit down where he was able to complete his talk. When he was finished, Dave walked offstage and collapsed next to Chris Carlson. He said, "Trade sweaters with me!" He didn't want anyone to recognize him on the way out. When the session broke for lunch, he all but ran from the auditorium.

At lunch, friends tried to reassure him. Although Dave rarely drank, he had a glass of wine with lunch to calm his nerves. Then he clicked into "classic Dave" mode. He was slated to do a second talk after lunch; he returned to the symposium—armed.

He took the empty jug of wine from which he'd had only one glass, stood at the podium, then said, "If you were here this morning, you'll remember something unique about my way of speaking. At lunch, I took it upon myself to get a little help." With that, he set the empty jug on the podium. It broke the tension. Mirth was Dave's go-to in stressful situations and it got him through the second presentation without incident.

Fear of public speaking haunts many people, including professional entertainers. Barbra Streisand threw up before most of her performances. Singer Adele admitted the same thing. When Donny Osmond starred in *Joseph and the Amazing Technicolor Dreamcoat*, an understudy had to fill in intermittently because Osmond suffered from panic due to stage fright. How could someone who had performed his whole life have this problem? A therapist helped Osmond understand that there was a definite environmental aspect to his anxiety: "He was judged as a young child; if he missed a step when he was dancing or he didn't hit a note or he wasn't funny enough . . . these were incredible pressures for anybody."[1] Osmond said, "There are times I remember where if I had the choice of walking on stage or dying, I would have chosen death."

Anxiety coach Janet Hilts described performance anxiety as a sort of post-traumatic stress disorder. "When you think of little kids in moderately normal homes, they love performing—you can't stop them," Hilts said. "Then some experience stomps out that enthusiasm. Some might have grown up in an environment where there was a lot of criticism, or maybe they were encouraged to be quiet."[2]

Dave fainted for the first time in eighth grade—he linked it to a critical comment from a teacher while he delivered a speech. Years later, he described it as a scarring situation. This likely set in motion a condition that plagued Dave into adulthood. However, there's more than the *psychological* aspect of Dave's stage fright to consider. There is the *physiological* part of the picture.

The vagus nerve extends from the brain stem to the abdomen by way of multiple organs, including the heart and lungs. This nerve is involved in one of the most common causes of fainting, called vasovagal syncope. The vasovagal response occurs when the body overreacts to certain triggers, which can be emotional or physical, such as standing too long or enduring excessive heat.[3]

When triggered, the vagus nerve impacts heart rate and blood pressure. As the heart rate slows, blood vessels in the legs dilate, which allows blood to pool in the legs and blood pressure drops. The lowered heart rate and blood pressure combine and reduce blood flow to the brain. The result is fainting. A common trigger for vasovagal syncope (also called neurocardiogenic syncope) is extreme emotional distress, such as seeing blood. In Dave's case, public speaking was his main trigger. Once the vasovagal response is triggered often enough, a vicious and embarrassing cycle can ensue.

Almost every person who knew Dave learned of his fainting condition. Those who witnessed his mishaps offer descriptions that fit with vasovagal syncope. Recovery after a vasovagal episode generally begins in less than a minute, which fits with the jack-in-the-box story about Dave. He was behind the podium, talking, disappeared, and in less than a minute, he popped back up.

Dave's fainting spells weren't only in response to emotional causes. His dad brought him and his sister for cancer screenings when they were both in their early twenties. Pat remembers, "Medical staff came and got me and told me that my brother had passed out. Then he threw up for the next three days."

Large-scale campaigns directed at early cancer detection gained momentum in the 1940s and 1950s. A frequent slogan was, "Delay kills!" One poster claimed that more people died from cancer every two weeks due to a delayed cancer diagnosis than had died at Pearl Harbor.[4] Tom Johnston lost both his parents at young ages and had lost a newborn daughter. He wasn't taking any chances. He brought Dave and Pat for cancer screenings that included a chest X-ray, proctoscopy, prostate exam for Dave, and blood tests.

After two consecutive years of Dave passing out during cancer screenings, Tom stopped insisting that he go. Luckily for the remainder of the American populace, the World Health Organization established criteria for screenings and examined the limits of early detection strategies—they asked, "Who is the target of the screening?" New guidelines dictated that otherwise healthy twenty-somethings did *not* need an annual workup of invasive screenings.

Overall, it was public speaking that made Dave faint, and he took a natural route to override his stage fright. He devoted ample time to rehearsal and preparation for presentations. He also admitted his vulnerability to his audience.

According to Janet Hilts, "You can release emotional discomfort by cracking a joke about being nervous." Dave did this at the GSA meeting when he placed the empty wine jug on the podium and poked fun at himself. By doing this, the audience connected with him because, as Hilts put it, he showed he was courageous enough to do something that might unnerve them—enlisting the crowd as your ally is key.

Still, Dave's shyness meant he hated moments when all eyes were fixed on him. When his professor assigned him the role of teaching assistant (TA) at the University of Washington, Dave showed up in the professor's office clearly rattled. He told his professor he was afraid he would faint. But being a TA was a requirement for his graduate degree; he had to get through it. He did well, even if he proved to be a pushover at times, such as when his class asked if they could ditch the lab exercises for the day and play volleyball instead—Dave's answer was . . . yes!

Dave beat his unease on many occasions—he didn't always hit the floor. Public speaking was one more obstacle to overcome.

The time came for Dave to defend his PhD thesis—to stand in front of his thesis committee and show what he was made of.

On the day of his defense, friends took matters into their own hands. As professor and thesis committee chair Stewart McCallum introduced Dave, two men suddenly appeared at the top of the stairs of the lecture hall. Without uttering a word, they carried a stretcher and set it up against the wall behind the podium. Others lined the aisle with medical bags. The audience was delighted, and the desired effect was not lost on Dave. The antics diffused his anxiety.

"His dissertation presentation was quite impressive," said University of Washington professor Steve Malone. "Dave exuded enthusiasm for geology in general and volcanology in particular." Dave had grown close to Malone, a seismologist who was head of the university's lab services. Two years later, Dave would join Malone in the lab to monitor a newly seismologically active Mount St. Helens— the beginning of much more to come.

After Dave finished his presentation but before he exited the lecture hall, he dedicated his PhD to his fallen friends who were killed during the Vietnam War, along with "all others whose opportunity to create was cut short by the war." Dave was acutely aware that the two men he had known since childhood would never stand on a stage to defend a thesis. They had performed a different sort of defense—through their service—and Dave spoke their names in memory and honor before they were etched into the Vietnam Veterans Memorial in Washington, D.C.

Dave's dissertation was an important contribution to the study of volcanic gases and added an important thread to a debate raging at that time about depletion of the earth's ozone layer. After chemists F. Sherwood Rowland and Mario Molina of the University of California–Irvine published—in 1974—the first scientific paper that warned that human-generated chlorofluorocarbons (CFCs) could deplete the ozone layer and recommended that CFCs be banned, industries that depended on CFCs attacked the theory. Doing away with CFCs was no small controversy; an estimate put the number at 3,500 uses—from refrigerants and appliances to electronics manufacturing and the auto industry.[5] CFCs fueled multibillion-dollar businesses.

Volcanic gas studies at the time focused on the presence of sulfur; however, Dave's analysis of emissions at Augustine showed that active volcanoes are capable of producing not just sulfur but chlorine. Soon, fingers pointed to volcanoes as a significant source of chlorine to the stratosphere. Not long after Dave's dissertation, on December 17, 1978, the New York Times interviewed Tom Casadevall, head of USGS's HVO gas lab at the time, to discuss chlorine's impact on the ozone. Key to the debate was the process by which chlorine is removed from gas in an eruption plume or stratosphere, something Dave addressed in an article he submitted to Science magazine in 1979 (published in 1980), where he asserted that it was not safe to assume that chlorine injected into the stratosphere by volcanoes would affect ozone concentrations in the same manner as those produced by humans.

Eventually, scientific research proved that the ozone is, in fact, impacted to a greater extent by anthropogenic sources of chlorine, much more so than from volcanic sources. Discovery of the Antarctic ozone hole in 1985 fueled more research, which led to the 1987 Montreal Protocol, where fifty-six countries agreed to cut CFC production. University of California's Rowland and Molina won the Nobel Prize in Chemistry in 1995 (which they shared with Paul J. Crutzen of the Max Plank Institute for Chemistry, Mainz, Germany).[6]

Dave's thesis paper was signed by the chair on March 8, 1978, and with that, he became Dr. David Johnston with a PhD in geology.[7]

Dave called his parents, and referring to his work at Augustine, he said, "Well, whatever else I do, I've left my footprint. This work puts one more link in the chain."

Dave's time at the University of Washington was circuitous and filled with hard work. It was also filled with love. Chris Carlson, whom he started dating in graduate school, became a serious girlfriend; eventually the time came to meet her parents.

They chose Christmastime for Dave to fly to her family's home in Houston, but something happened on the way there. The plane ride gave him hours to think about the big family gathering that lay in wait. "Meeting a bunch of my friends and family was a big move for him," said Chris. "I grew up in a fairly boisterous, extroverted family. He had the whole flight to think about it and worried, 'What if they don't like me?'" His flight landed, but Dave didn't exit the plane.

When there was no sign of him, Chris started to leave. Then she spied him, flanked by two stewardesses giving him a pep talk: "Of course her family will like you." Dave caught sight of Chris and felt a bit better. He had anticipated rejection, but of course her family loved him. He and Chris went running every morning of the visit and the routine helped.

Dave had survived Mount St. Augustine but was intimidated by a bunch of spirited Texans. A few years later, he told his sister he thought he'd reached a point where he could find something to talk about with almost anyone.

Dave actually loved to talk. Whether he would open up depended on the situation.

One of his graduate professors said, "Dave would begin talking as soon as he entered my office and continue for several minutes before I could get a word in edgewise."

While in Alaska, Dave came across a few tourists and captivated them with his explanation of the 1912 eruption in the Valley of Ten Thousand Smokes.

Dave Johnston and Chris Carlson. Photo
courtesy of the Johnston family.

A childhood chum described Dave as just one of the guys . . . shy when dating, but day-to-day, he was fine.

Dave absolutely had the gift of the gab—something every person of Irish
descent supposedly possesses. It's a trait he would have inherited from his dad,
who loved to spin a good yarn. Dave kept his chatty side in check when he felt
unsure, but when he felt relaxed, it was as though he was standing atop the
Blarney Stone.

Dave had visions of his life after college, and it definitely involved stones—but
not the kind found at an Irish castle. Even though he wanted very much to work
for the Geological Survey, he thought it prudent to apply for a faculty position at
Stanford. Much to his dismay, he passed out during the interview. Dave thought
he had the fainting under control. It surprised him as much as anyone when it
happened. A person on the selection committee said this was *not* the reason he
wasn't hired.[8]

Stanford didn't hire Dave, but USGS came through. He was thrilled to start
the next chapter of his life.

DARE TO LIVE THE LIFE YOU HAVE
DREAMED FOR YOURSELF.
GO FORWARD AND MAKE YOUR DREAMS COME TRUE.

Ralph Waldo Emerson

6

DREAM JOB

WHAT INSPIRES A PERSON to work around active volcanoes and run inside craters hot enough to melt boots? Innate curiosity is definitely part of the equation. Dave's curious nature meant he was willing to commit effort toward deeply cherished goals despite distress and tension. Behavioral researchers define this as being psychologically flexible.[1]

Curiosity goes hand in hand with cognitive flexibility, or openness to think outside the box. Dave illustrated this trait after Augustine's eruption when he retrieved a plastic paper towel holder that melted inside the shack on the island. He wanted to know the temperature of the hot cloud released from the volcano. So he bought the exact replica of the plastic holder, then experimented with it in an oven until it drooped in the same manner. The results of Dave's "droop test," as he called it, were innovative, and according to his thesis chair, Stewart McCallum, the audience he presented it to found it "impressive as well as entertaining."

Once Dave finished his class work at the University of Washington, he moved to the San Francisco area, where he worked seasonally for USGS's regional office in Menlo Park. By the time he successfully defended his PhD, his work with volcanic gases caught the eye of USGS and he was hired in 1978. He was offered a "career conditional" appointment through Menlo Park to expand their program for monitoring volcanic emissions in Alaska and the Cascades of the Pacific Northwest.[2] Federal jobs such as his came with a period of probation before consideration for a permanent position. Dave was intent on proving himself.

Tom Casadevall was the only other USGS geologist besides Dave at the time who analyzed changes in the chemistry of gas emissions as a means to understanding volcanic processes. Tom was hired by USGS in 1978 to set up the first ever volcanic gas lab at the Hawaiian Volcano Observatory (the only volcano observatory in the United States at the time). A friendship between Dave and Tom began during the mid-1970s in the San Juan Mountains while they were working on their own projects. Their lives intertwined as USGS employees performing basically the same role; they talked by phone frequently.

To be a volcanologist is to set aside fear and take measured risks in order to advance the understanding of the earth's processes, some of which can be deadly if misunderstood. Tom talked about risk-taking: "While pursuing my career, I didn't necessarily think about the hazards of working around volcanoes. That's like saying it's dangerous to get in the car—while driving, if you run a red light you'll put yourself in big danger. When a volcano is in a state of unrest, it's sort of the red light. You have to be aware of the warning signals."[3]

Dave, Tom, and others took risks, but taking risks does not make one reckless. If that were the case, we would have no firefighters, police, military, search and rescue teams, or roofers (roofers were ranked fourth on a list of the most dangerous jobs in 2014).[4] High-rise buildings would be grimy with no one to climb onto a suspended scaffold forty stories high. We'd have no organized football teams without those willing to risk concussions; many argue this *is* a reckless career for entertainment's sake. We'd also have no Alaskan crab without deep-sea fishermen—the second most dangerous job in the world. And first on the list: logging. The wood that forms your desk, table, or house is the product of the most dangerous job in the world.

Some questioned Dave's risk-taking. Volcanologist Barry Voight spoke about what he observed: "Dave certainly wasn't reckless. He did work he was hired to do in the interests of both science and public safety, but with an unusually full appreciation of the risks."[5] Voight, a world-renowned geologist and landslide expert from Penn State, crossed paths with Dave at Mount St. Helens in 1980.

An elite and rare breed, the exact number of volcanologists worldwide is difficult to determine because the field is comprised of many different geological sciences. However, the International Association of Volcanology and Chemistry of the Earth's Interior (IAVCEI), the main professional organization for volcanologists, has around 1,500 members. Of those, the number of people who monitor and work on active volcanoes is much more limited and is probably only, at most, several hundred people.

For Dave, the pursuit of volcanology started with a geology class in college. Others dream much sooner of entering the field. A geologist from New Zealand described her first inkling: "When I was young, I dreamed of working around volcanoes but thought, 'That is way too cool for a real job.' Then at thirteen, my teacher spoke about volcanoes and volcanologists and I literally sat back in my chair and thought, *This is what I am.*" Another geologist knew from age eleven that geology was "it" because of a childhood spent around mountains—specifically Dinosaur National Park, which straddles Utah and Colorado (a park Dave also visited as a kid with his family).

Dave's job with USGS put him in harm's way; however, he had great respect for the terrain in which he worked. He loved his job and was proud of his association with the Survey. To his parents, he exclaimed, "I can't believe they're paying me to do this job!" Climbing around active volcanoes may not seem like a dream come true, but for Dave it was. His aptitude, curiosity, and energy fit the job description. Performing the physical work he craved, contributing to science that could make the world safer, he was in his element.

Dave was called a walking encyclopedia of geology by a deputy director with the U.S. Department of Energy (DOE) after his assessment of geothermal resources in Portugal and the Azores Islands in late 1979.

From Roman baths to root cellars, humans have tapped into the earth's natural energy for thousands of years. When it comes to heat, the best geothermal prospects are associated with active or geologically young volcanoes such as those found on the Azores archipelago. Made up of nine volcanic islands, the Azores is an autonomous region of Portugal located 800 miles (1,300 kilometers) west of the mainland. Even though the islanders had great potential for harnessing the warmth below their feet, they had struggled for direction in geothermal energy before Dave arrived on the scene.

According to the DOE, Dave combed the islands and acquired a "total understanding" of their needs and capabilities. He then sat with the Azores director general of energy and their top experts and helped map out their geothermal energy future. Dave was thanked not only by the DOE but also by the U.S. State Department, who said he had helped with a matter of state—"a very critical and sensitive issue." Afterward, the Azoreans requested follow-up studies based specifically on Dave's analysis.[6]

Although initial interest in geothermal development in the Azores began decades earlier, the first exploratory well wasn't drilled until 1974. Following Dave's meeting with officials in November 1979, a 3MWe pilot plant* was installed in 1980 on the largest of the Azores Islands—São Miguel—near the Pico Vermelho cinder cone. (Regional Director of Energy Deodato Sousa would write to the Johnstons after Dave's death to tell them that Dave's name will remain "attached to the new era of energy in the Azores.")

Thirty-five years after the first plant was installed, power production from geothermal resources was meeting 42 percent of electrical consumption on the Azores's largest island of São Miguel and meeting over 22 percent of the total demand of the entire archipelago.[7]

When Dave wasn't traveling, he truly enjoyed California living with its laid-back lifestyle. His job at the USGS office in northern California meant that most of the time no suit or tie was required—unless of course he was meeting with Azorean top officials.

When a cousin from Ireland got married in Los Angeles in 1979, Dave donned a linen suit—all the rage in California at that time. But his attire raised his parents' eyebrows. When questioned, he defended his selection: "It's California casual. . . . Everyone here wears this."

That Christmas, Dave became the proud owner of not one but two leisure suits—hints from his parents. One of the suits was light blue with dark blue stitching. Message received? Yes, loud and clear.

California living had other advantages. Dave was near Stanford, where he engaged in some research. Also, he was near Chris Carlson, who moved there to attend Stanford. They continued to date on and off. But his thesis work had kept him away, especially when he switched the focus and extended his time at the University of Washington. The geographic separation took its toll. Marriage talks started and stalled. While shopping together, Chris found a tunic with a

---

* 3MWe stands for 3 megawatts of electricity output capability.

Pictures taken during Dave's fieldwork in Portugal, 1979. Photos courtesy of Johnston family.

beautifully embroidered vest and Dave told her she should buy it. When she asked where she would wear it, his reply was: "To our wedding." They also bought a wedding tie for Dave. Their plans twisted in the wind, the romance ebbed and flowed, but one thing continued—their friendship.

"Dave had a great sense of humor," said Chris. "We were both at USGS and it was his thirtieth birthday. I arranged for various females in the office to call his desk throughout the day and purr into the phone, 'I've been thinking of you. ... I hope you have a happy birthday.' Then they hung up. For days, he tried to identify who they were. He enjoyed jokes . . . he never took himself too seriously."

That was Dave's last birthday. Chris and others infused it with fun. What a gift, friendship.

Dave lived and worked in California, but he spent considerable time in Alaska. One of his first projects as a new USGS employee was to take part in a comprehensive study of the Novarupta volcano complex.

The twentieth century's most voluminous volcanic eruption was in 1912, and for years it was attributed to Mount Katmai, just six miles from Novarupta. The area is remote, uninhabited wilderness, located on the Alaska Peninsula, which extends five hundred miles (eight hundred kilometers) southwestward from the mainland. The rugged terrain made it hard to reach. Frequent storms stirred up ash and dust. Add bears to the mix and it is clear why it took until 1953 for geologists to discover that it was not Katmai but Novarupta that erupted over a sixty-hour period in June 1912.

Following the eruption, thousands of fumaroles puffed steam into the air. Its appearance was that of the communication system used by indigenous people— smoke signals created by fire and blanket. Thus, the area became known as the Valley of Ten Thousand Smokes.

Dave made the two-week trip to Novarupta in summer 1978 with Dan Kosco, who was pursuing his doctorate at the University of California–Berkeley and had previous research experience in the area. The two covered much ground together. It was on this trip that Dave enraptured a group of tourists with the tale of the 1912 eruption.

Dave and Dan posed for a photo in the Valley of Ten Thousand Smokes— each was suspended by ropes on either side of a rock bearing the etched initials

Dave at Novarupta in 1978.
Photo credit USGS.

of early explorers. Most copies of the picture show only a smiling Dave—Dan
has been cropped off, but he appears in the weathered and peeling copy that
hangs on his office wall.

During the trip, Dave sampled fumarolic gases at several volcanoes besides
Novarupta, including Mageik, Griggs, and Trident. He also devoted energy to
improving the equipment and techniques for collecting gas samples; he didn't
like to waste time or effort on contaminated or compromised specimens. When
scaling mountains, wasted time equates to wasted energy, and wasted energy
can be a threat.

Another threat is the challenge of toting enough food into the field. Geologists' backpacks are filled with sampling gear, sleeping bag, and tent, which
doesn't leave room for much else. One day while transporting heavy rock

samples, Dave hiked more than three hours to a cabin near Mount Katmai. At one point, he retrieved a sandwich from a trash can that had been discarded by a tourist. Luckily, one of Alaska's dangerous denizens hadn't targeted the trash can before Dave got there . . . or targeted Dave.

A very real threat, specifically in Alaska, is that of the unexpected bear. When Dave told Pat that USGS was instituting firearm training to guard against bear encounters, he expressed serious doubt that a shotgun would save him—he said he'd have a better chance of survival if he broke the gun in half and stuck it up the bear's orifice. His qualms had more to do with the type of weapon rather than the use of firearms in the field. In the early days of USGS training, instructors taught that a shotgun would provide the best defense in southeastern Alaska, which wasn't the case. A rifle or handgun provides greater accuracy—and it is good for distance. That last part is especially important; you want distance between you and a bear that is hunting you. Waiting until the bear is close enough to get a good shot can spell disaster. Eventually, it became clear that out on the ridges a shotgun was not the best choice.

The firearms training came about because of an alarming case of a USGS geologist who was mauled by a black bear while performing fieldwork in Alaska during the summer of 1977. Cynthia Dusel-Bacon, who also worked out of USGS–Menlo Park, survived the attack but lost both her arms.

Years after USGS started training geologists to carry firearms in the field, a rifle saved the life of USGS geologist Marti Miller. While performing fieldwork, she found herself being stalked by a black bear. Like Dusel-Bacon, she was alone. Miller radioed for the project helicopter but it was out of range. The bear continued to stalk her, closing the distance, and she had to take action. A bear can sometimes run after being shot, but Miller was lucky. The bullet entered the bear's neck and severed the spinal cord. It dropped, and she escaped unscathed.[8]

Others have not been so lucky. Although bear attacks are considered rare, four people in Alaska were mauled in June 2017. Two were killed, including a sixteen-year-old runner participating in an annual race near Anchorage. Authorities say that race time should be the safest period in which to run along the path because heavy traffic would normally keep bears away. But the black bear that attacked Patrick Cooper was hungry. When Cooper realized he was in trouble, he texted his family that he was being chased by a bear. Unfortunately, he didn't know to stand his ground with a black bear; running triggers its predatory instincts. Playing dead with a black bear also doesn't work.

This is why USGS conducts training (and provides geologists with bear spray, which saved two of the people attacked in June 2017). When a park ranger found Cooper's body, the bear was guarding its meal. The ranger shot the bear in the face and it ran away. *It ran.* This was Dave's point; shooting a bear won't necessarily save your life.

In summer 1979, Dave returned to Alaska for a thirty-day stint with a team of USGS geologists, including Wes Hildreth. Hildreth was a fellow USGS staffer with plenty of experience at Novarupta. He had been trained in firearms and was "packing" on that trip; Dave was unarmed.

In addition to being colleagues, the two men had become running mates and good friends. Hildreth described Dave's "agility, nerve, patience, and determination around the roaring jet from Mageik's crater lake" as an unforgettable sight.

One of Dave's samples at Mageik measured 172 degrees Celsius (341 degrees Fahrenheit). By overcoming fear and taking measured risks, Dave proved that he was a valuable asset. As his probationary period with the Survey neared its end, he was offered a permanent position to start a volcano hazards program in Alaska.

Dave had mixed feelings about moving to Alaska. It was an opportunity to continue his research on his beloved volcanoes, but it also meant being isolated from the rest of the scientific community. Don White's story is an illustration of isolation, and Dave would have heard about it since Dave and Don both worked at Menlo Park and worked as part of the same team in Alaska in 1979. Don was a pioneer in geothermal research and geochemistry and had worked for years in a one-man USGS office in Carson City, Nevada. Scientific contact was limited to mail; when Don moved to Menlo Park, he loved the "exciting intellectual environment amidst a wide spectrum of earth science experts."[9] His experience demonstrates the value of proximity. Dave enjoyed alone time, but he also thrived on relationships.

Dave knew Cynthia Dusel-Bacon from Menlo Park; her tragic ordeal would still have been fresh in his mind. Bears would be one more danger to contend with in Alaska. In addition, adding geographic distance from his friends and family may have figured into Dave's hesitation to move to Anchorage. He hadn't lived near his family since he was seventeen, and distance had strained his relationship with Chris.

Dave had a long discussion with colleague and friend Darrell Herd about whether he should accept the position.[10] Dave knew the job was one countless others would be honored to have been offered. Once again, Dave struggled with what he wanted versus what he needed. He *needed* a permanent position with the USGS.

Several days after Dave spoke with his friend about the job offer, he decided to accept. Herd said Dave seemed pleased. Even though he still had qualms, he had worked hard to prove his worth to the Survey and this was a chance to solidify his career with them.

He was to transfer out of his position at Menlo Park and report to USGS's Branch of Alaskan Geology in Anchorage on June 1, 1980.

ASHES WERE ALREADY FALLING . . . A DENSE BLACK CLOUD
SPREADING OVER THE EARTH LIKE A FLOOD . . . DARKNESS
FELL, NOT THE DARK OF A MOONLESS OR CLOUDY NIGHT,
BUT AS IF A LAMP HAD BEEN PUT OUT IN A CLOSED ROOM.

**Pliny the Younger,
witness to the eruption of Mount Vesuvius, 79 AD**

PART THREE

FIRE MOUNTAIN

SO HE CLEANED OUT THE EXTINCT VOLCANO, TOO.
IF THEY ARE WELL CLEANED OUT, VOLCANOES BURN
SLOWLY AND STEADILY, WITHOUT ANY ERUPTIONS . . .
ON OUR EARTH WE ARE OBVIOUSLY MUCH TOO SMALL
TO CLEAN OUT OUR VOLCANOES. THAT IS WHY
THEY BRING NO END OF TROUBLE UPON US.

Antoine de Saint-Exupéry

7

FOLKLORE AND HISTORY
OF MOUNT ST. HELENS

MUCH WAS NOT KNOWN ABOUT VOLCANOES IN 1880. In a report that year on the high plateaus of Utah, volcanologist Clarence Dutton said, "The origin of volcanic energy is one of the blankest mysteries of science, and it is strange indeed that a class of phenomena so long familiar to the human race . . . should be so utterly without explanation." Dubbed the "poet of the Grand Canyon," Dutton was known to indulge his imagination when thinking about the earth.[1]

Humans have historically used storytelling to understand natural phenomena for which they do not have an explanation. Vulcan, the god of fire, is a mythological figure whose forge was located under Mount Etna in Sicily.

In the sixteenth century, Masaya Volcano erupted as explorers conquered Nicaragua, and for the next hundred years many believed that Masaya was the Mouth of Hell.[2]

In North America, First Nations peoples developed beliefs about Mount St. Helens. The Klickitat called it Tahonelatclah, or Fire Mountain.[3] The Cowlitz called it Lavelatla (name variations include Lawilaytla or Lawelata), which means Smoking Mountain.[4] And the Puyallup called the mountain Loowit (short for Loowitlatkla, which means "Lady of Fire").

Mount St. Helens in 1978. Photo credit U.S. Army Corps of Engineers.

Their stories were passed down through generations to explain blazes and vapor that emitted from the earth, sometimes violently.

According to Puyallup legend, Loowit was a wrinkled old woman who faithfully tended the fire of the mountain and was kind to those who came for embers to build fires for their villages.[5] For all her hard work, Loowit was granted one wish by Chief Sahale. She wished for youth and beauty. When Sahale granted her wish, his two sons both fell in love with Loowit and fought for her affection; in the process, they burned forests and villages. Sahale became so angry that he smote all three. Where each lover fell, Sahale raised up a mountain. Because Loowit was beautiful, her mountain was a dazzling, symmetrical cone—Mount St. Helens. Sahale's two sons became Mount Hood and Mount Adams. Together, the three made up a lovers isosceles triangle.

Star-crossed lovers who morph into mountains are not the only subjects of local lore. There is also the furry figure walking upright through the forest, as has been viewed in fuzzy video footage. Speculators wonder if it is an alien or species of animal unknown to humans. Bigfoot, sometimes called Sasquatch, is the fabled apelike humanoid who purportedly walked the terrain of the area for decades. Strange and enormous footprints were pointed to as proof.[6] And whenever new footprints were found, tourism spiked. One local man, Harry R. Truman, owner of Mount St. Helens Lodge, perpetuated the fable. Truman's niece said her uncle carved a pair of big wooden feet so that he could make the prints in fresh snow himself; it was good for business.[7] Local newspapers printed stories of the spring mating dances of the Bigfoot, dances that caused the mountain to shake and rattle along with the waltzing.

Locals say Bigfoot died in the 1980 eruption of Mount St. Helens. Just west of the volcano in front of the North Fork Survivors Gift Shop, a twenty-two-foot statue stands as a memorial to the legendary enigma.

Another local legend recalls the bandit Dan Cooper (also called D. B. Cooper). In 1971, Cooper hijacked a domestic flight then parachuted from the rear stairway of the plane somewhere over southwest Washington near the Cascades. Some say he landed safely and lived out his days in the Mount St. Helens area. No one can say for sure what happened; it remains the only unsolved case of air piracy in FBI history. What is known is that Cooper parachuted at ten thousand feet in a storm . . . at night . . . in blustery November . . . wearing a trench coat and dress shoes. Some theorize that he died in the eruption—along with Bigfoot.

A discovery in early 1980 added more mystery. A bag of twenty-dollar bills, about one-fourth of the $200,000 Cooper had with him when he jumped, was found along the Columbia River near Vancouver, Washington.[8] The serial numbers matched those in Cooper's possession. More credible than the hijacker's survival is the idea that somewhere in a creek bed that feeds into the great Columbia River lie his remains, along with a trench coat and dress shoes.

A member of the British Navy greatly influenced the Pacific Northwest. Captain George Vancouver set sail for the area in 1792 to assume control of the territory assigned to England by the Nootka Convention—an agreement between Britain and Spain.[9] Upon arrival, Captain Vancouver dubbed the beautiful peak formerly known as Tahonelatclah, or Loowit, Mount St. Helens in honor of the Baron St. Helens, Alleyne FitzHerbert—a fellow countryman and British ambassador to Spain at that time.

Vancouver was no neophyte to exploration. He had joined the Royal Navy at fifteen and served under Captain James Cook, joining Cook's famous around-the-world voyage from 1772 to 1774.

Vancouver explored and mapped the north Pacific coast, and his maps later informed and encouraged U.S. president Thomas Jefferson to fund a westward expedition to find a long sought northwest passage to the Pacific Ocean. Jefferson gave the task to explorers Meriwether Lewis and William Clark, and they set off in 1804. Although they failed in their mission, they reached the Pacific and established an American presence in the Pacific Northwest; this was important because of previous claims by European countries, including Great Britain.

The struggle for control of what became known as the Oregon Territory (present-day Oregon, Washington, and most of British Columbia) came down to America and Great Britain, and by the 1820s they were at a stalemate. Great Britain wanted the northern border of the United States to follow the Columbia River (latitude of forty-five at Portland, Oregon, to forty-six where the river meets the ocean); however, America's stipulation was the forty-ninth parallel. Decades passed with no resolution; as American immigration to the Oregon Territory increased, the two countries finally agreed on the forty-ninth parallel, which is the current latitude that separates the western United States and Canada.

Vancouver's name shows up along the north Pacific coast today. Vancouver Island, part of British Columbia, shelters a busy seaport. Also, two cities are named for him—one in Canada and one in the United States. In Vancouver, Washington, on the second floor of the Forest Service building, the USGS set up a temporary office when Mount St. Helens began to quake in 1980. Vancouver would later become the permanent location from which to monitor the Cascades volcanic range.

People thought Mount St. Helens was beautiful, perfect for skiing, no threat whatsoever. Volcanologists who had studied the area thought differently.

What seems like a long time to humans is a geological eyeblink. Most of the visible part of Mount St. Helens's beautiful symmetrical cone in 1980 was formed over the preceding thousand-year period.[10] It is a composite volcano, or stratovolcano, which means that it took many eruptions over time to form. With each eruption, layer upon layer of emitted rock, lava, and ash was added, increasing its size and height until its elevation reached 9,677 feet (2,949 meters).

Prior to 1980, geologists were hard at work identifying past eruptive stages that formed St. Helens. Their work traced three hundred thousand years and four stages: Ape Canyon, Cougar, Swift Creek, and Spirit Lake.[11] Each stage was separated by dormant intervals and left its own geological footprint. Before the current eruptive stage (1980 to present), the most recent stage was called Spirit Lake, which geologists broke into "eruptive periods"—the youngest of these, the Goat Rocks period, lasted fifty-seven years and its last eruption was in 1857. Then came the dormant period that masked its destructive potential. Although the Goat Rocks period didn't significantly change the appearance of the mountain, erupted tephra and andesite flows (viscous lava) formed the Goat Rocks dome and set the stage for what followed.

93

The Cascade Range is part of the Pacific Ring of Fire, a near-continuous chain of volcanic arcs, ocean trenches, and sites of seismic activity that runs along the edges of the Pacific Ocean. Four hundred fifty-two volcanoes stretch from the southern tip of South America north along the North American coast, cross the Bering Strait, and run south past Japan down to New Zealand. Of these, eighteen of the Cascades' volcanoes have been active within the past two thousand years, and seven have been active in the past two hundred years.

Prior to Mount St. Helens, Mount Lassen in Northern California was the last to erupt in the conterminous forty-eight states. Located midway between the California/Oregon state line and Sacramento, California, Lassen awakened as the twentieth century dawned.

A steam explosion in 1914 signaled a new eruptive stage for Lassen, and it rumbled intermittently over the following year. Then on the evening of May 19, 1915, as area residents settled in for the night, an explosion shattered the dome and ejected glowing blocks of hot lava.[12] Thirty feet of snow blanketed Lassen's peaks and contributed to an avalanche of snow and rock that traveled four miles down its steep flanks. As the snow melted, the avalanche morphed into a giant mudflow, or lahar.

A barking dog awoke a slumbering homesteader, who saw the approaching wall of water and warned neighbors. But Lassen saved its most powerful explosion for three days later—rock fragments and pumice lofted high into the air and a column of ash and gas rose thirty thousand feet (nine thousand meters). A pyroclastic flow* devastated three square miles (seven and a half

---

* A pyroclastic flow is a dense mass of hot ash, lava fragments, and gases ejected from a volcanic vent that flows downslope at high speed.

square kilometers), a lahar rushed fifteen miles down Lost Creek, and ash drifted two hundred miles east.

There were close calls for inhabitants of several ranches in the path of flooding, as well as for scientists, photographers, and sightseers in the area. Despite Lassen's destruction, its death toll was zero.[13]

The next Cascades volcano would erupt sixty-five years later, almost to the exact date. There would be similar hazards—lahars, pyroclastic flows, ashfall, and a "tree blow-down zone"—but from the standpoint of human lives, the outcome would be drastically different.

NATURE, LIKE LIFE, STRIPS MEN OF
THEIR PRETENSIONS AND VANITIES.

W. Macneile Dixon

8

THE AWAKENING

TWO PIONEERS DECLARED MOUNT ST. HELENS to be the most active and explosive volcano in the conterminous United States. Volcanologists Dwight "Rocky" Crandell and Donal Mullineaux worked in the Cascade Range for years before issuing a 1978 report that was largely ignored.

Because Mount St. Helens hadn't erupted since 1857 and Lassen was a distant memory, the government had little incentive to increase research funding. Lack of a sufficient budget was a perennial problem, which hampered efforts of geologists to advance the science. The 1978 report would turn out to be a harbinger.

Crandell and Mullineaux of the USGS Volcano Hazards Program in Denver wrote: "Mount St. Helens' lack of recent activity, and our limited knowledge of volcano behavior . . . preclude our knowing what kinds of premonitory events and which monitoring techniques will provide the most reliable warning." They continued: "The volcano's behavior pattern suggests an eruption is more likely to occur within the next hundred years, and perhaps even before the end of this century."[1]

A warning with a twenty-two- to one hundred–year time span didn't grab the public's attention, although some agencies convened meetings to discuss the hazards that the report described. When the volcano awoke in March 1980, the geologists' twenty-five-page paper became required reading for all government officials, public-safety organizations, and anyone with a vested interest in the area.

Mount St. Helens awoke from its 123-year nap with a stir and a stretch. On March 20, 1980, a moderate magnitude 4.2 earthquake shook the area, and seismologists determined that it was shallow and located immediately northwest of the summit.[2]

Seismology is integral when monitoring volcanic hazards; the seismic network that monitored St. Helens was run by the University of Washington. The head of the university lab was thirty-five-year-old seismologist Steve Malone, who immediately notified USGS of the quake and its aftershocks. It was decided that additional seismometers should be installed in the area to increase monitoring capability.

Then on March 22 there was a second moderate-size quake, along with many smaller ones. Seismologists determined that it wasn't just one quake with aftershocks; the St. Helens area was experiencing a series of earthquakes called a swarm. A day later, there were six quakes. The next day, fourteen. By March 25, there were twenty-five earthquakes—an average of one per hour; but the "average" belied the big picture. Five quakes (magnitude 4 or greater) occurred within an hour's time, and twenty-two of the twenty-five occurred within an eight-hour window. Things were heating up rapidly.

The U.S. Forest Service manages the Gifford Pinchot National Forest around Mount St. Helens, thus decisions about closures fell to them. With the growing number of earthquakes, the Forest Service closed areas above the timberline and warned residents of possible earthquake-induced avalanches.

Dave was at a meeting a few hours from Seattle when he heard about the rumbling. Rather than return home to California, he drove to the University of Washington to see Malone and volunteered to help. Malone put him to work in the lab counting earthquakes.

"Dave was excited and asked questions," said Malone. "Up to that point, what was going on was of interest to seismologists, but Dave sensed something bigger."[3]

Earthquakes dwell in the world of seismology, but when quakes occur at a volcano . . . in great number . . . and they're close to the surface, it suggests that magma is rising from inside the earth. This is why Dave took notice. Conditions seemed to indicate that volcanic hazards could follow. One such hazard overtook an area around Dieng volcano (Indonesia) in 1979; carbon dioxide (CO_2), heavier than air and slow to dissipate from low-lying areas, was emitted from a distal fissure, flowed downslope like an invisible river, and killed 142 people. Even though St. Helens isn't heavily populated like Dieng, gas emissions is still a volcanic hazard to keep an eye on.

Dave stayed the whole week and it paid off from the viewpoint of volcanology. Seven days after the first earthquake—on March 27—Mount St. Helens exploded with a burst of steam and black ash. Dave was so excited that he did a little jig down the hallway with Steve Malone's wife. Every volcanologist dreams of viewing—from a safe distance—an eruption. Dave saw the activity at the mountain as an unparalleled opportunity.

A few reporters were already in the area due to the earthquakes and closures in the Gifford Pinchot National Forest. When the volcano spewed ash and steam, more swooped in. They wanted to know, *Was the mountain about to blow?* There was no USGS office in the Cascades at the time, so few volcanologists were available. The press called Malone for an interview; they offered a free ride over the volcano as an incentive to lure him from his lab. But he felt his responsibility was to stay put and watch further seismic activity. Instead, Malone offered the reporter a "real volcanologist"—David Johnston.

Dave flew with the news crew, and from the air he saw that the explosion had bored a small crater into the peak's summit. He also noted large cracks in the glaciers on the north side of the mountain, which he thought could indicate magma rising inside the volcano.

The helicopter landed at Timberline viewpoint on the flank of the mountain. Suddenly Dave was surrounded by reporters. Concern for public safety fueled his courage and he spoke frankly about the possible hazards as he understood them.

"We stand at a dangerous place," said Dave, like "standing on a keg of dynamite and the fuse is lit, but we don't know how long it is."

On cue, the mountain rumbled. The reporters looked to Dave for further comment: "If it were to explode now, we would die."

Dave continued: "The more earthquakes there are the more worried I get."

There was plenty to worry about. Seismic activity had increased so much

Dave and reporter Jeff Renner. Photo courtesy of Jeff Renner.

in a week that a half-dozen earthquakes (magnitude 3.5 or higher) per day
was the new normal. Fifty-seven quakes were recorded the day Dave did the
interview—the ground seemed to quiver continuously.

After a narrow escape two years earlier at Mount St. Augustine, Dave felt
the danger of a steaming, trembling volcano at experiential and visceral levels.
Following is another of Dave's interviews:

> In the initial phases, we'd probably see large eruptions that would ex-
> tend high into the air. This would spread ash over large areas in western
> Washington and maybe, in an extreme case, even farther east. On the near
> flanks of the volcano, there would be more damage done by possibly hot
> avalanches, pyroclastic flows. Farther downstream, we could see mudflows
> and floods. Because this is such a symmetrical volcano and because the
> crater is so high, if there's an explosion, it's probable that the debris, the
> very hot incandescent ash that would come down, could come down all

sides. But right now, there's a very great hazard due to the glacier's breaking up on this side of the volcano, the north side, and that could produce
a very large avalanche hazard.[4]

Dave's words would prove to be eerily insightful. Even so, he was cautioned to
be careful when dealing with reporters. Five years earlier in March 1975, another
Cascades volcano ominously heated up; there were closures, and then . . . nothing. Mount Baker, located at the northern edge of Washington state, exhibited
a major change in steam activity—a situation that can signal a volcano is in a
state of unrest. USGS increased monitoring efforts.[5]

The Forest Service, responsible for public safety in the area, formed a task
force. The task force recommended closing areas around Baker's summit. Potential hazards included a massive mudslide from high on the volcano's slope
that could enter Baker Lake and send a wall of water into campgrounds. Public
areas remained closed through the summer, a time of year when local businesses
depended on tourism dollars. Nine months later, after no eruption, no mudflow,
and no large-rock avalanches, the Forest Service reopened Baker's public areas.
Those who lost income blamed the USGS, even though they hadn't made pre-
dictions nor were the closures their decision. When Donal Mullineaux heard
about Dave's interview, he asked him to be cautious with the media.[6] Senior
USGS geologists recognized Dave's commitment to warn the public; however,
they wanted consistent messaging.

Dave couldn't help feeling unsettled; he'd been honest about the possibilities
he thought could come to pass. He didn't mean to scare anyone unnecessarily.
He later wished he hadn't used the dynamite analogy, but it's what came to his
mind during the interview.

Soon, many non-USGS scientists were in the field, each with different expertise and experiences—and many were doing interviews. Conflicting information
gushed, and there was no shoring up the dike.

One supposed expert who made inflammatory statements was Frenchman
Haroun Tazieff, who toured the area and pronounced the USGS incompetent.
He said it was the "God-given right" of the public to see the volcano.[7] (USGS had
denied Tazieff's request to sample gas at St. Helens; they had enough scientists
already, but thanks.) There were other voices; anyone with a geology degree
seemed to have an opinion.

USGS geologists came to Vancouver from various locales—from Denver came Rocky Crandell, Donal Mullineaux, Dan Miller, and Rick Hoblitt. All were part of USGS's Volcano Hazards Program.

Since people needed information at all times of the day and night, USGS decided a spokesperson should be available around the clock to coordinate communications. Crandell, Mullineaux, and Miller divided each twenty-four-hour period into three eight-hour segments. The geologists handled press conferences, as well as meetings with federal and state agencies, law enforcement, landowners, residents, and others. "At times, there were three meetings a day," said Dan Miller.[8]

Scientists' immediate concern was to determine whether Mount St. Helens's activity had a magmatic cause, and if so, how close the magma was to the surface. They needed a sample from the volcanic vent that had ejected hot ash and steam.

Don Swanson took on the task. Swanson, a red-haired, forty-two-year-old volcanologist from the Hawaiian Volcano Observatory (HVO), asked a helicopter pilot to fly him to the summit. In a spine-tingling maneuver, he used a ladle attached to a yard stick to scoop ash as the helicopter hovered. But the sample didn't suggest the presence of magma.[9]

Subsequent explosions blew more than ash and steam—the volcano spit rocks three feet wide into the air. Scientists rushed to collect samples—results showed pulverized old rock, as opposed to juvenile rock, which would indicate the presence of magma.

Of the dozen explosions on March 28, one lasted two hours. Geologists determined that earthquakes, many of which were growing stronger, were centered beneath the volcano at a depth of less than one mile. Then on April 1, the seismology lab at the University of Washington detected a harmonic tremor—a wavelike ground fluctuation often associated with magma on the move under the earth's surface.

USGS wanted to keep their eyes on the volcano from dawn to dusk. Initially, they set up posts on both the north and south sides of the volcano. Then Crandell and Hoblitt scouted for an observation post using the 1978 hazard zone map from the Crandell/Mullineaux report. Eight and a half miles northwest of the summit near the mouth of Coldwater Creek, they scratched into the sides of the walls of a ridge looking for sediment layers that would reveal its history.

Dave uses a hand lens (magnifying glass) to examine rock samples taken from near the crater of Mount St. Helens on March 23, 1980. Photo credit Johnston family and USGS.

They didn't find evidence that a lethal event had occurred on the ridge in the past, so a tent was pitched and the post was dubbed Coldwater. Time-lapse cameras were installed and geologists took turns at the post. With logbooks and radios, they reported what they saw to USGS staff in Vancouver.

A week after the March 27 burst, Washington governor Dixy Lee Ray appointed a Mount St. Helens Watch Group and declared a state of emergency.[10] Hundreds of people were evacuated from homes, logging camps,* and public areas. She also called upon the National Guard to enforce roadblocks.

Main roads were closed within a fifteen-mile radius of the summit, but a web of logging roads crisscrossed the mountain, which complicated efforts. Even with sixty National Guardsmen to aid local law enforcement, there wasn't enough

---

* Timber was a major industry.

manpower to block all arteries that led to possible danger. Despite warnings, it soon became apparent that many people wanted, if not a front-row, at least a middle-row seat to the Mount St. Helens show. "People are swarming in from all over, putting their lives in danger," said a Washington Emergency Services staffer. "When the weather was clear, the road up to the mountain looked like downtown Seattle at rush hour."

As more reporters and tourists converged on the area, hotels and inns filled up. Dave stayed at a hotel in downtown Vancouver, an almost two-hour drive from the mountain. He shared his room with colleagues—the floor was better than a sleeping bag in the cold. Everyone just needed sleep, especially after rigorous workdays that often lasted fourteen hours.

Thrill seekers from as far away as New York came to see the volcano huff and puff; they were able to purchase maps that showed how to get around blockades. "There was a competition to see who could get closest," wrote Vancouver's *Columbian* reporter Bill Stewart. "Some people actually landed on the crater rim and climbed inside."[11] A group climbed to the top and filmed scenes intended for a documentary—and for a beer commercial.

A newspaper headline touted: "It's Exciting, Fun: Hawkers, Gawkers Jam Roads." Below the headline was a man with long hair, glasses, and a smirk, who climbed to St. Helens's summit on April 3 (just six days after its first explosion of ash and steam) and peeked inside the crater. As a freelance writer, he hoped to sell his story.

Dave had stayed on at Vancouver rather than return to Menlo Park, and like every other volcanologist, he was excited to be there. But it was more than that. Many eruptions begin and end with gas emission, and Dave's specialty was volcanic gas studies.

Tom Casadevall flew in from the HVO shortly after March 27. Since Dave and Tom were the USGS "gas guys" and Dave had a new assignment in Alaska coming up, they discussed their schedules. They agreed there was no way to tell how long it would take to figure things out. Since Dave was supposed to be in Anchorage on June 1, Tom said he would return home to Hawaii in mid-April, then he would come back to St. Helens about mid-May to relieve Dave. This would give Dave time to pack up his apartment for his big move.

Dave using gas equipment in spring 1980. Photo credit Johnston family and USGS.

A blue flame inside the summit's crater on March 30 tantalized the imaginations of the gas guys. Although burning gas had been observed above lava flows at other volcanoes, there was no previous record of it inside a crater *before* lava erupted. Dave reasoned that this indicated the presence of a flammable gas. He thought the glow was likely from combustion of sulfuric gases that emerged from the volcano's vent(s)—at high pressure and temperature, gas could ignite when it came into contact with air.[12] But before the flame's cause could be determined, it disappeared three days later and was never spotted again.

The lack of time and knowledge prevented scientists from deciphering all they saw. It was frustrating, exhausting, and exhilarating.

Geologists had various tools at their disposal.

A tiltmeter network measured even the slightest changes in uplift of ground surface. The tiltmeter as well as the geodimeter were designed to detect ground deformation. If magma moved toward the surface, the ground would move, or deform, as well.

The geodimeter measured the distance between two points. A laser beam emitted from the geodimeter would hit a target, then return to the recording device. If the time taken for the beam's roundtrip shrank, this meant the distance between the two points was shorter also. Geologists placed targets at varying points on the flanks of the mountain and took frequent measurements with the geodimeter. A target on the north side grabbed their attention.

From Timberline in late April, Peter Lipman found that a target at Goat Rocks had moved three yards in two days. At first, he chastised himself—had he forgotten how to measure? But the numbers were correct. A mile-wide stretch of rock bulged outward from St. Helens's northern flank.

Like the frog in water that doesn't notice as the water comes ever so slowly to a boil, scientists hadn't noticed—visually—the growth of the mountain's new blemish, or "bulge." Starting around the time of the initial activity in late March, a cryptodome* had formed and the north flank began to push outward. Magma had risen miles from beneath the mountain, flowed through its central conduit, or "pipe," and was struggling toward the surface at the summit's central vent

---

*A cryptodome is a pocket of magma that intrudes into a volcano's edifice but doesn't erupt at the surface.

The bulge on the north flank; view from northeast. Photo credit USGS.

(opening at the surface). But something stood in its way—a cork of sorts—and it kept the rising magma bottled up within its edifice.

Dave kept an eye on gas readings, which remained low. If levels spiked, that could warn of an imminent eruption. He learned to use the Correlation Spectrometer (COSPEC) on the flanks of St. Helens, a tool designed to measure pollution, which also *remotely* detects levels of sulfur dioxide (SO_2).

Since SO_2 can dissolve in groundwater, and there was plenty of water on the volcano, including snow and ice, scientists realized that low gas readings could be off. During a sustained lull in eruptive behavior in mid-April, Dave rode in a helicopter that landed at the crater's rim to *physically* obtain a gas sample. Those results showed low levels too.

USGS geologists thought a sample of the water from the pond at the bottom of the summit crater might provide different or more accurate readings. But who would go?

Dave using the COSPEC. Photo credit USGS.

Dave volunteered for the task. As a strong runner, it was as though he had trained for this moment. He figured he could make it in and out as fast as anyone on the team, and it was, after all, gas readings they were after.

During a period of relative quiet from the mountain, he dashed down into the 150-foot-deep, 350-foot-wide crater (45 meters deep, 106 meters wide). Results from this formidable excursion also showed that gas levels remained low—much lower than expected if an eruption was on the horizon.

News reporters wrote about Dave scrambling into the summit crater; back in Oak Lawn, his parents read about it. When they next talked by phone, Dave tried to downplay the feat: "Aw, that wasn't so much," he said. "You know how these newspaper guys are."

Dave climbing down into the summit crater to test pond water at the bottom. Photo credit USGS.

Mount St. Helens was cracking. From east to west across its peak, two fractures formed with the onset of steam and ash explosions and continued to grow. They spidered down the northeast and northwest flanks of the mountain as though slicing a chunk of pie.

Geologists worried about the cracks because flank failure could result. And failure of a peak of almost ten thousand feet could produce a fast-moving land-slide of epic proportion.

Rocky Crandell asked landslide expert Barry Voight to assess the cracks. Barry was a geologist and professor at Penn State University who resembled his actor brother, Jon. Barry arrived on the scene in mid-April and camped near the

Coldwater post to study the mountain. He saw that the distribution of cracks indicated that the north slope had moved sideways, and that the movement was continuing.

Since this behavior was consistent with a possible impending flank failure, Barry returned to Vancouver and immediately relayed his thoughts to Rocky Crandell. "I told him that if the north slope failed in a landslide, any magma deep in the edifice would be depressurized . . . and that could cause an explosion. Water vapor in the magma would immediately boil from the great pressure reduction, causing a nearly instantaneous explosion that could also have a lateral component and generate a pyroclastic flow."[13]

Then Barry sketched a north-to-south section of the mountain that showed a landslide failure on the north slope. He wrote on the drawing: "Magma Pocket— boils when surface load removed suddenly—possible trigger for pyroclastic event."[14]

Rocky was in a meeting with the Forest Service when Barry caught him on a break and relayed his assessment. Rocky returned to the meeting and explained the possibility of a flank failure as a significant hazard—a hazard with *no warning*.

At that point, Barry Voight's assessment was based on his observations. Several other outcomes were possible. Nothing about Mount St. Helens was definitive.

Since a composite volcano is made of material from past eruptions, the growing bulge on the north flank was a conglomeration of hardened lava, rocks, and ash. As magma muscled its way toward the surface, more cracks formed on the north flank. The glaciers atop Mount St. Helens began to melt from the heat, and this added to the instability of the 450-foot (140-meter) bulge that towered thousands of feet above its base.

USGS director William Menard visited St. Helens in mid-April, and Donal Mullineaux accompanied him on a car ride to Timberline viewpoint. Located on the northeast flank, two miles from the summit, Timberline afforded a full view of the bulge.

Mullineaux's historical visual knowledge of St. Helens was based on many years of research. He immediately realized the volcano was grotesquely disfigured. Though Mullineaux was continuously in the area since late-March, he hadn't stood on St. Helens's flanks for the preceding two-week period. From viewing aerial pictures, he hadn't realized how much change had taken place.

"When I got out of the car and looked at the bulge, I was shocked . . . frightened," he said. "I wanted to be gone from there as soon as I could."[15]

Where Menard and Mullineaux stood would be completely demolished a month later.

"Dave was the first person I heard talk about a lateral blast," said Tom Casadevall.[16] "But we didn't know. Geology 101 teaches that volcanoes explode *up*."

Dave and Tom had dinner with various geologists in mid-April. In a mischievous moment, Dave and Tom signed the restaurant's guest register with fake names. Dave used a fictitious name and wrote, "No it won't!" and Tom signed Dave's name, along with: "Yes it will!"

This story was related as a way to suggest that Dave *knew* St. Helens was going to blow. Dave *felt* an eruption was imminent. But no one had unequivocal answers.

At dinner, Dave brought up Bezymianny volcano (called Bezy), located on the Kamchatka peninsula in Russia. Bezy is 1,680 miles (2,700 kilometers) from Mount St. Augustine, a part of the world in which Dave spent ample time. Bezy was considered extinct until it surprised everyone when it erupted in 1956.

Georgii Gorshkov, a leading figure in mid-twentieth-century volcanology, researched Bezy, and his 1959 report described the phenomenon of a directed blast. The Gorshkov/Bezy report was one of many that filled Rocky Crandell's fat file of literature on explosive eruptions in 1980. Although not all of Gorshkov's assessments were correct, he was the first to describe this type of volcanic hazard.

With a directed blast, the shallow magma inside a cryptodome can suddenly depressurize and allow rock and gas to rapidly reach the surface. If the easiest or least resistant path is laterally through the volcano's flank—versus upward through its main vent—then that is the route it can take. Kind of like a gun, the explosion will shoot out the side of the volcano. This is what happened at Bezy, and Dave thought the conditions at St. Helens were similar.

"We do take risks working so close," said Dave. "It could surprise us. . . . St. Helens will likely erupt magma, but it may take time. Bezy had months of minor action like this before its 1956 burst."[17]

Dave brought up Bezy at a staff meeting.[18] His natural propensity was to avoid speaking in front of large groups, even with colleagues, especially those with much more experience. So Dave armed himself with his favorite tool—humor. He said he had a guest speaker, then he produced a toy dinosaur; sparks came from its mouth.[19] Dave felt more comfortable once levity was employed. The dinosaur made it easier for Dave, a junior scientist, to add his thoughts.

USGS geologist Richard Waitt attended the dinner where Dave spoke about Bezy. Like Dave, Richard was from USGS–Menlo Park. He had been in the middle of mapping ash layers in the North Cascades when Mount St. Helens first stirred in March. After the dinner, Richard decided to track each time the volcano's bursts started and stopped, the height of its jets, and other volcanic activity he gleaned from logbooks and field notes. As he reviewed reports of Lassen and Bezy, he found that patterns of early activity at both explosive volcanoes resembled what was occurring at Mount St. Helens, and he thought, *David Johnston is right.*

But too much was unknown at the time. Comparison to Bezy was considered conjecture.

April disappeared and tourist season loomed. USGS held a meeting with owners of lodges and youth camps, law enforcement, and various government agencies.

Crandell told them, "A large quake or steam blast could send a 150-foot ice mass careening down at 180 miles an hour." With a tidal wave twelve-feet high, there would be no way to warn people. Crandell made it clear: he could not say when, only that it was a very real and dangerous possibility.[20]

The YMCA, Boy Scouts, and Girl Scouts had permanent camps at nearby Spirit Lake; the mountain towered above them. All three organizations agreed not to open for the season. Lodge managers also agreed to stay shuttered. Fishing season, however, had already begun. Tourists were doing their thing, fishing and camping, using roads that were not closed but within the potential frontier of danger.

Mount St. Helens's eruptive and seismic activity slowed down in late April. It went from three explosions of steam and ash on April 5, to an explosion that lasted five hours on April 8, and several major and minor explosions on April

10, including multiple harmonic tremors (one lasted thirty-two minutes)—to a sudden lull. No explosions were recorded on April 20; there was minimal activity in the days that followed.

The lull caused media to ask whether the previous weeks had been a bit of short-lived histrionics. Headlines hinted that the hubbub might be over. Dave responded: "Lassen in California went through a year of this kind of activity before it turned into a magmatic eruption in 1915."[21]

Local businesses were hurting. Stan Lee, owner of the Kid Valley Store twenty miles from the peak, complained about road closures that kept away customers. He scoffed at talk of an explosive and far-reaching eruption. A newspaper photo of sixty-seven-year-old Lee showed a broad-shouldered man in a black collared shirt and suspenders; he held up a cast of Bigfoot's alleged footprint. Lee's protests joined others, which succeeded in getting the roadblock moved a few miles closer to the mountain; customers were able reach his store again. People had to make a living.

Roadblocks were put in place early on but more were needed. The Forest Service didn't have proper jurisdiction to keep people out of certain areas; they needed a state directive, so they sent a proposal to Governor Ray and asked for two zones of protection.

On April 30, Governor Ray issued an executive order that designated a Red Zone, roughly five miles around the summit (including Spirit Lake). The Red Zone was closed to all except law enforcement and volcano monitoring.

Another area, the Blue Zone, would be open to daytime logging operations. Those whose job it was to enforce closures inside the national forest were dismayed when the Blue Zone they requested to the west of the mountain's summit was lopped off.[22] With the executive order, the roadblock in place a month earlier was moved closer to the mountain.

The governor had to weigh the scientific information presented to her. It was impossible to predict the timing or magnitude of any potential hazard, and there were economic factors to consider. Ray felt a compromise was reasonable.

The two zones defined by the state were the only enforceable boundaries. Where road blockades were moved closer, Captain Richard Bullock of the Washington State Patrol instructed troopers only to check the steel gates at dawn and dusk to ensure they were locked but not to stand guard in the shadow of the bulge.

Dave joined the effort to deter sightseers from crossing into certain areas. When he found a family on a logging road, he advised them against being there. Dave seemed to get more passionate as time went by. In early May when he found a father and his daughters too close to the volcano, Dave gave the man a stern lecture; he told him to leave and not come back. Then Dave waited as the man piled his kids into their car and pulled away. One of the daughters remembered an "amazing twinkle" in Dave's eye as he looked from the volcano to the retreating car; then he gave a wink to her dad as a way of saying: *That's right, keep going!*

One of Dave's coworkers from USGS–Menlo Park said Dave talked of spending a lot of his time chasing away sightseers. There were roads that afforded views of St. Helens that Dave clearly felt might turn out to be dangerous. Part of the problem was dubbed the Truman Effect. While others were kept out of the Red Zone, lodge owner Harry Randall Truman was given a permit to come and go. Many wondered, *Why him and not us?*

When the mountain started quaking and people were evacuated, eighty-three-year-old Truman* refused to budge. He had lived for fifty years at Spirit Lake in the shadow of St. Helens, where he and his wife, Eddie, owned a lodge. After Eddie died in 1975, he became increasingly reclusive.

Truman's rantings gave the media a local celebrity. A newspaper printed a picture of him with the caption, "Give 'em hell Harry!" In the picture, he held two sacks of groceries and a stock of whiskey that he said kept him going.

Performing for reporters, Truman shook his fist and roared, "I'm not afraid of that mountain!" He talked of dropping a bomb into the volcano's crater.[23] He rose to folk hero status. People sang songs about him. A fifth-grade class in Oregon wrote him letters, and the media helicoptered Truman to the school for an appearance. The children thought he was brave for taking a stand.

Truman even received a letter from Governor Ray, in which she praised him for his "independence and straightforwardness."[24] She said politics could use a lot more like him. He got a kick out of the notoriety, but St. Helens had lessons in store for those who decried its danger.

---

* No relation to President Harry S. Truman.

Law enforcement and friends tried to persuade Truman to leave. County officials didn't want to remove him forcibly since it would raise questions about their jurisdiction. The St. Helens area was a mixture of federal and privately owned land. There was a national forest bordered by timber companies as well as land owned by the Burlington Railroad.

As earthquakes shook his feet and the walls around him, Truman was adamant. He wanted to stay put with his endless supply of whiskey and sixteen cats. "If I left this place . . . if I lost my home, it would kill me in a week."[25]

Truman didn't care for the assessments of geologists. When asked about Dave Johnston's metaphor that the volcano was a dynamite keg with a lit fuse, Truman responded, "That's just poop."[26] During a visit with Richard Waitt and Barry Voight, he spouted that geologists didn't know "shit" about what was going to happen at Mount St. Helens.[27]

The violent rumblings of the volcano did indeed scare the old curmudgeon, but rather than say so, he criticized the work of experts and promised to go down with the ship like an old sea captain. The media lapped it up, and Truman became stuck with his image. The Cowlitz County sheriff said that after all the press, Truman thought he would look silly to leave, especially if nothing ended up happening.

Even as the ominous bulge pushed out from the volcano at a steady pace, northward toward his lodge, Truman didn't sway. Some felt his grandstanding might influence others to jump onto the defiant bandwagon. Seeing him come and go through roadblocks did indeed cause people to question the gravity of the situation.

The "frightening and shocking" bulge continued to grow, and laser measurements documented its daily movements.

Peter Lipman told how from the point of view of monitoring, geologists expected to see an increased rate in certain things. They believed there would be a flank failure on the north side, but first they expected to see some sort of spike—in volcanic gas, for example, or in the speed of growth of the bulge. But gas readings remained a fraction of that detected before magmatic eruptions at other volcanoes, and the bulge didn't increase its velocity. Like the turtle in the race, it moved slow and steady . . . northward.

On May 1, USGS chose a different ridge for its main observation post. The new post would be on the opposite side of Coldwater Creek from the original; it was nine hundred feet higher and about two and a half miles closer to the volcano, which would allow more accurate laser measurements.

Crandell and Hoblitt inspected the ridge, and as with the first observation post, they did not find evidence of lethal volcanic activity. Despite this, Crandell voiced reservations; he felt something in his gut and said—*I have no proof, just a feeling that a tragedy will occur here.*[28]

The new observation post was 5.7 miles north-northwest of the summit, just outside the state-designated Red Zone, and was dubbed Coldwater II. The original post then became Coldwater I. Equipment was moved to the new post along with a travel trailer. Coldwater II was to be manned twenty-four hours a day; the trailer would provide shelter from nighttime elements.

Dave had hired Harry Glicken to be his field assistant in Alaska for summer 1980. Glicken was pursuing his PhD in geology at the University of California–Santa Barbara. With all the activity at Mount St. Helens, Dave asked him to come to Vancouver instead of Alaska. Almost immediately after Coldwater II opened, Glicken was sent there to record observations.

Glicken was a twenty-two-year-old quirky and spirited grad student with dark hair and wire-rim glasses. He was inexperienced but proved to be a sponge and soaked up lessons from his new mentor. Some said "Harry's habits" hid a certain brilliance—he might drive right through stop signs while absorbed in a conversation, but his ability to focus on meticulous details showed up in his work. He did well at Coldwater II and remained there almost continuously for two and a half weeks.

The first week of May brought gentle behavior from the mountain, comparatively speaking. It steamed but it did not explode. Also, the number of earthquakes slowed.

Then on May 12, geologists spotted a new cluster of fumaroles on the western rim of the summit crater. The next day, they saw new steaming areas on the west side just outside the crater rim—evidence of melting glaciers.

On May 14, levels of SO_2 were reported to be much higher than samples collected in March. Elevated SO_2 could correlate with magma moving closer to the surface.

Meanwhile, logging crews worked in the Blue Zone and there was talk that the road to Coldwater II might be blocked for timber purposes—it was, after all, their road. Worried about Glicken, Dave placed a call to the Air Force Reserve in nearby Portland to notify them of the presence of a scientist on the ridge; Dave asked if they could provide air support if the escape route became blocked.[29] They said they could, but Dave still worried.

USGS staff stood sentry and analyzed changes taking place at Mount St. Helens. Discussions and debates broke out as quickly as analyses were conducted. They hoped to be able to warn of something that, at the time, was unforeseeable.

Only one of Alice's children was in the Chicago area on Mother's Day—May 11, 1980. The other one was monitoring a volcano. Dave and Mount St. Helens posed for a Polaroid picture together and it reached Alice in time. Across the white strip at the bottom, in big black letters, Dave wrote: "Hi Mom!" In the photo, it's hard to see blond Dave with his full red beard.

A small sheet of gold Shilo Inns Hotel letterhead accompanied the photo. On it, Dave scribbled a short note: "It looks like this volcano may erupt soon and I'll be around here for a while. I'm afraid, or maybe not afraid. It'd sure beat Anchorage."

There is much contradiction in so few words. Dave previously told his parents, "I hope they don't take me off the mountain before it erupts." And he told the media, "We all (volcanologists) want to stay. We don't want to be in California or Denver or Virginia if something happens."

Dave was exhausted, and yes, he was afraid—like other volcanologists who were part of the team there—but it's where he wanted to be. He wasn't stuck on a remote volcanic island in a blizzard with limited resources as with his first brush with an active volcano. At St. Helens, he was within driving distance of civilization and he was surrounded by experts with various monitoring equipment.

When Dave called home on Mother's Day, Alice was busy so father and son talked—and exchanged "I love you"s—until Alice was ready to greet her son. Dave told his parents that being at St. Helens was the opportunity of a lifetime. He also talked to Pat; he told her that some people seemed to consider him an alarmist. "He sounded annoyed, he felt stifled, and down too," said Pat.

Glicken wanted to be wherever Dave was; he looked up to his mentor. Dave worried about Glicken's inexperience in the face of surrounding dangers; he didn't like his continued presence at Coldwater II. Eventually, something tugged Glicken away from the St. Helens area—he needed to travel to Santa Barbara to meet with University of California geology professor Richard Fisher about pursuing his doctorate.

As the weekend of May 17–18 approached, Glicken planned for his time away. Don Swanson was going to take over at Coldwater II for the few days Glicken would be gone. Then Swanson received a request from a friend—a professor whose grad student from Germany would be in the area—could Don show him around?

Swanson looked for someone to take his place at Coldwater II for one night— the night of May 17. He asked Dave, who had reservations but was committed to his job. He said yes, and the two agreed that Swanson would relieve Dave the next morning.[30]

Then came the lull. Three days passed without explosions of steam or ash. Minor earthquakes continued but at a lower rate. The bulge, however, didn't slow down; it continued its steady rate of growth.

During what appeared from the outside—outside USGS that is—to be a safe period, residents asked to retrieve belongings from their mountain cabins. A few threatened to gather and storm the barricades. On Saturday, May 17, with Governor Ray's consent, fifty carloads of property owners were escorted to their cabins. Each signed a liability waiver and promised to leave by nightfall.

Another caravan was scheduled to go into the Red Zone the next day, on Sunday, May 18, at 10:00 a.m.[31]

Dan Miller had contacted the military at Fort Lewis in Tacoma and arranged to have an armored personnel carrier brought to Coldwater II.[32] He wanted it parked so that the viewing ports were aimed toward the volcano.

"By then we knew deformation was on the north side," said Miller. "We knew there could be a large avalanche and a magmatic eruption." They thought a person could survive an eruption in the carrier. Delivery was scheduled for the morning of May 18.

Despite lack of evidence, Dave's feeling that the volcano would blow in "hours, days, maybe a couple months" (in his words) never wavered. He wanted to

118

help decipher the conundrum of Mount St. Helens and he saw gas readings as an important puzzle piece. So with three preceding days of relative quiescence from the volcano, with cabin owners trekking into restricted zones, with his own presence scheduled on a nearby ridge that night, and an armored car scheduled for delivery the next day, Dave hitched a ride in a chopper to the crater's rim. He wanted more gas samples.

Since a cluster of new fumaroles had been discovered a few days earlier, perhaps he thought they would provide the high gas readings he expected to see. While standing on the crater's rim, an earthquake shook the ground. With samples in hand, Dave nervously called for the chopper to come back for him. Those were the last pre-eruption samples taken at the summit crater.

Dave called Chris Carlson every evening the week before the eruption. On Saturday, May 17, he sounded drained during their phone call.[33]

"Field work is physically and intellectually exhausting," said Chris. "You're collecting and trying to understand your samples. Dave was worried. He sensed that an eruption was imminent. When he called that last night, he was on his way to relieve Harry Glicken at Coldwater II."

It was late Saturday afternoon when Dave drove to the ridge dubbed Coldwater II. The two men were there together when two women showed up. Mindy Brugman was a Caltech grad student whose research project was on the glaciers that covered Mount St. Helens, and Carolyn Driedger was a hydrologist with USGS-Tacoma. It's a good safety protocol to perform work with a partner—Driedger and Brugman were friends, Driedger was helping out.

The women had their camping gear and planned to stay on the ridge for the night. Dave said no and insisted they return to the safety of their hotel—there was no reason to put more than one person at risk.[34]

Brugman grew up skiing and climbing the mountain and knew it well. Besides, other scientists swarmed the area performing their research; she wanted to know why she shouldn't stay.[35]

Dave answered, "There's a chance that the ridge isn't safe." Driedger was doubtful—surely it couldn't reach them five and a half miles from the summit.

"Yes, it could," said Dave.

The geologists had had some fun at Coldwater II. They took turns sitting in a director's chair, arms outstretched, waving back and forth as though conducting a symphony. They played at directing harmonic tremors, ash clouds, and the eruption to come.

Driedger and Brugman departed around 7:00 p.m. Before they left, Dave suggested they attend the 7:00 a.m. staff meeting in Vancouver the next morning. He wanted them to hear updates directly, and Brugman could present her case for obtaining a helicopter to observe the glaciers.

At about 9:00 p.m., Glicken prepared to leave also. He promised Dave he'd be back the following weekend, but Dave wanted him in Menlo Park with some samples.[36] Was Dave trying to waylay Glicken's return? After all, he had spent more time than anyone at Coldwater II.

Glicken departed and Dave was left alone on the ridge. He had twelve hours until Don Swanson was due to arrive the next morning. There was fresh mountain air and a trailer to catch a few winks. There was also concern. There's no way to know if Dave slept that night. One thing for sure, he was up with the sun the next morning, taking more readings.

"I LOVE YOU, DAD."
"I LOVE YOU TOO, DAVID."

Dave and Tom Johnston,
phone call one week before eruption

9

MAY 18, 1980

EACH PERSON WHO REMEMBERS MAY 18, 1980, would write this chapter differently.

As you read these sections, know that details of this day are written purposely concise. Extensive writings on the science appear elsewhere; the survivors' tales have been told, obituaries written. For each word here, know that a million more would not do justice to what happened that day. The heart defies vocabulary.

Dave was up at sunrise and radioed Vancouver just before the regularly scheduled 7:00 a.m. staff meeting. He reported the results of three laser measurements he took at 0553, 0623, and 0653 (5:53 a.m., 6:23 a.m., and 6:53 a.m.).

Bob Christiansen was at the radio in Vancouver that morning. Christiansen was a senior USGS geologist who had worked at Yellowstone in the 1960s and later moved to the Menlo Park office. He took note of Dave's early morning work, then asked about the weather. Dave described the day as very nice, perfectly clear, temperature about ten degrees Celsius (fifty degrees Fahrenheit).

When Christiansen asked if Dave detected any SO_2, in Classic Dave fashion, he answered with a joke . . . no, but there's an internal buildup of H_2S (a gas emitted from volcanoes . . . also present in human flatulence).

Dave referred to the four samples he took the previous day at the crater's rim. He had tried to determine the pH of the condensate, which appeared neutral—this suggested low levels of SO_2. He said the fumaroles were 87 degrees Celsius (188 degrees Fahrenheit), not pressurized, and he could smell H_2S.

Then Dave ended his last detailed report with, "Vancouver clear, I mean, Coldwater clear." The next "report" would be a radio transmission that lasted mere seconds. Words heard round the world: "Vancouver, Vancouver, this is it!"

At 8:32 a.m. (PDT), a 5.1-magnitude earthquake caused the bulge on the north face of the mountain to give way and the largest landslide in recorded history sped down its flank. As the north side of the mountain slid down, a blast of hot gas and rock shot out, and reached Coldwater II . . . and Dave.

In the distance, a volunteer observer for the Washington Department of Emergency Services, Gerald Martin, radioed that the camper and car on the ridge south of him were covered—he was referring to Coldwater II. Martin saw the blast cloud; then he said it was going to get him too. It did.

Meanwhile, Reid Blackburn, a twenty-seven-year-old newlywed with a full red beard and glasses, was on assignment from the *Columbian* newspaper in Vancouver, Washington. He was on loan to the *National Geographic* and was taking pictures from Coldwater I—the original observation post eight miles from the summit. Four feet of ash from the blast blanketed the ridge, and Blackburn's new wife, Fay Blackburn, became a widow. And his parents became childless; he had been their one and only.

There is a difference between a landslide and an avalanche; however, in the case of Mount St. Helens, the two terms are used synonymously to describe what happened. An avalanche occurs when snow or rocks detach from a mountainside and slide down. A landslide occurs when the side of a mountain—the land mass that makes up the mountain—slides down. Mount St. Helens was a composite volcano; its "land" was made of lavas, pyroclastic debris, and glacial deposits that collected in layers over centuries. Ice from the glaciers melted and added to the avalanche, and what occurred was, according to USGS, "a huge landslide—the largest debris avalanche on Earth in recorded history."[1]

Each eyewitness saw something different and yet the same—abrupt, massive, deadly devastation.

Eruption column; aerial view from southwest. Photo credit USGS.

Dan Miller was on his way to Coldwater II. The armored car was scheduled to be delivered and he wanted to be there when it arrived.

"It was a beautiful blue-sky day," recalls Miller. "I was driving up Interstate 5 . . . and as I glanced over at the mountain . . . suddenly I saw this mushroom-shaped cloud go up above the volcano and climb rapidly into the stratosphere."[2]

If a helicopter had been available that morning, Miller would have made a quick hop from Vancouver to the ridge and he would have seen the beginning of the eruption from Dave's viewpoint.

Carolyn Driedger and Mindy Brugman attended the 7:00 a.m. staff meeting and then headed back to Mount St. Helens.

"We were driving on I-5 and could see the debris avalanche from the side angle," said Driedger. "It looked like this big black rolling cloud. And we thought, 'Whoa, what is that?' It took a few moments for it to dawn on us what it was—it was a debris avalanche, a possibility Dave had talked about the night before. We kept thinking, 'Well, it doesn't look like any eruptions we've seen in the past . . . there's a little spitting from the summit.' We thought maybe it was one of those big Slash Burns. But it kept moving, and it was going to the north, and that was our clue. We just couldn't believe it. It was so beyond our experience."[3]

Keith and Dorothy Stoffel happened to be in nearby Yakima, Washington, to attend a gem and mineral show. As geologists with a few free hours that morning, the Stoffels hired a pilot. On their fourth pass over the mountain, they saw its side start to slide down, a sight they described as rippling and churning movement. The debris avalanche had begun, and its surface undulated like ocean waves as it crashed down the north flank.

People on the ground experienced a rainfall of pumice. Of those who thought they were a safe distance from St. Helens, some were able to retreat, others not. Some careened down mountain roads with hairpin turns to outrun hot ash clouds. Survival came for many due to a combination of strength, skill, and luck.

In eastern Washington, people heard reports of the eruption; however, St. Helens had been spewing steam and ash for weeks so those at an outdoor event at Fairchild Air Force Base weren't worried. Then a gray mass moved rapidly toward them. The skies turned dark, ash started falling, and people ran for cover.

Removal of the bulge essentially uncorked the volcano, and massive amounts of hot rocks and scalding ash shot out like bullets from a machine gun. Geologists later determined that it was a directed blast—directed *laterally* from its disintegrated north flank.

The directed blast traveled at speeds up to 400 miles per hour (643 kilometers per hour). It leveled most vegetation within 12 miles (19 kilometers) in a

180-degree arc to the north.[4] And it devastated an area that stretched nearly 19 miles (30 km) from west to east.

Within an inner zone extending nearly 6 miles (10 kilometers) from the summit, a once dense, old-growth forest was gone.[5] Just beyond this area, all standing trees, some 100 feet tall, were blown over and lay in piles like toothpicks. And at the blast's outer limit, trees were thoroughly seared—their outside surfaces were black and scorched.

Hot debris carried by the blast severely damaged 230 square miles (600 square kilometers). For perspective, that is roughly the same size as Chicago. Envision the skyscrapers of downtown blasted away and a moonscape in its place. The seventy-seven neighborhoods that comprise Chicago would be razed; from Rogers Park to the north, to O'Hare Airport to the west, and south to Hegewisch, which touches the Indiana–Illinois state line. The border towns that ring Chicago, including Oak Lawn, would see the damage from their backyards.

Volcanic directed blasts are among the most devastating of natural phenomena. In 1980, their dynamics were not well understood. Since then, much has been learned about the origin, effects, deposits, and other aspects of this volcanic process; but there is still more to learn.[6]

What was once nicknamed the Mount Fuji of America—a majestic snow-clad mountain—was now transformed into a wasteland.

Once Mount St. Helens's main conduit was exposed, a massive eruption of tephra (ash and rock fragments) shot twelve miles into the sky—called a Plinian eruption because of its similarity to Mount Vesuvius's eruption in 79 AD. At Vesuvius, Pliny the Younger described the mushroom-shaped cloud that blotted out the sun and turned day into cloudless, moonless night. His uncle Pliny the Elder was a naturalist, writer, and naval commander who died in the eruption along with an estimated two thousand residents of Pompeii, Italy, which was built in the shadow of Vesuvius.

It is estimated that Mount St. Helens's blast released 24 megatons of thermal energy, equivalent to 1,600 times the size of the bomb dropped on Hiroshima.[7] And its Plinian cloud resembled the one that grew over the Japanese city in 1945.

For nine hours, numerous pyroclastic flows poured from St. Helens's newly formed summit crater. Ash fell downwind and drifted hundreds of miles. Eventually the ash circled the globe.

The once 9,677-foot tall, symmetrical mountain was reduced by 1,300 feet—it lost enough material during the eruption to fill 1 million Olympic-size swimming pools.[8]

The snow and ice that had hugged the volcano began to melt after the initial blast ejected hot rocks and scalding ash. The resultant water led to destructive lahars.

The consistency of wet concrete, lahars poured down the Toutle River valley to the west and reached speeds up to sixty miles per hour (ninety-six kilometers per hour). They continued fifteen miles downriver, carrying trees, knocking out bridges—and in the path lay Kid Valley.

The debris-filled wall of water and mud missed the main section of Kid Valley but reached outlying areas, leaving up to twelve feet of mud in its wake. A half-buried A-frame house still stands as testament to the horror of that day.

An account of the lahars' impact on the Toutle included fish leaping out of the water because of rising temperatures. A young couple camped along the South Fork Toutle riverbank was sucked into the lahar and nearly drowned. They escaped but sustained significant injuries.

Many others in the area also managed to escape, but reports of the missing poured in. Family and friends anxiously awaited word about loved ones.

Search and rescue teams in helicopters took to the skies. Pete Holmberg was a captain and platoon leader for the Washington Army National Guard's 541st Aerial Attack Helicopter Company. He was also a former aeroscout in a cavalry unit in Vietnam. According to Holmberg, the Vietnam vets "knew how to improvise." His unit performed most of the rescues on that first day, as well as in the period that followed.[9]

Chopper pilots and their crew performed feats that were nothing short of miraculous. Landing meant stirring up layers of ash, which could (and did) choke up engines. As in a war zone, many were saved despite extremely dangerous conditions. In all, two hundred people were plucked from surrounding areas, including a family of four camped thirteen miles north of the summit with their two young daughters; one was four years old, the other just three months old.

Heroes dangled from cables in order to reach victims. The critically injured were transported to hospitals, where some would remain for months to heal.

Buried A-frame in Kid Valley; the balcony marks the second story of the structure. Photo courtesy of R. L. Holmes.

Harry Glicken and others searched for Dave. Glicken could not sit still; the idea that Dave might be hurt and needed him was overwhelming. No sooner would a helicopter return Glicken to the ground than he'd talk another pilot into taking him up. The terrain had changed so much it was hard to find where Coldwater II had been. Carolyn Driedger described Don Swanson returning from his first search mission over the area—Don was "white as a ghost."

Driedger and Brugman had returned to Vancouver; the phones in the make-shift office of the USGS rang nonstop. Both women began answering calls. Someone asked them to assemble talking points; they didn't know the terminology so they wrote what people told them. "We did this all day," said Driedger. Eventually, others arrived and took over.

By the evening of May 18, twenty-four hours had elapsed since Glicken, Driedger, and Brugman stood with Dave on the ridge. The three hugged as they realized how close they had come. Even though they were physically and emotionally spent, they stayed up all night together. There was talking. There was journaling. And there were silent prayers.

Glicken was awash with the thought, *It should have been me.* And Driedger and Brugman were overwhelmed with gratitude for Dave's direction to return to Vancouver. "If it hadn't been for who Dave was, telling us to leave, we'd be dead," said Brugman.

The night of May 18, and for nights to come, the hotel where Dave had been staying kept his room secure for his possible return. Officially, he was "missing."

MORTALITY IS A GAME OF MUSICAL CHAIRS.

Anna Quindlen

10

AFTERMATH

WASHINGTON WAS DECLARED A STATE OF EMERGENCY. Interstate 5 west of the volcano was nearly severed, as was an Amtrak rail line. Debris flow brought transportation on the Columbia River to a halt and almost blocked cooling-water intakes at a nuclear power plant.[1]

Three hundred fifty miles (five hundred sixty kilometers) east of Mount St. Helens, Spokane was draped in complete darkness. Motorists were stranded by poor visibility or disabled cars, and people shuttered themselves inside homes to avoid respiratory distress. Many shoveled ash by garbage can loads and quickly became ash-fatigued.

Major ashfalls also occurred in Montana. Visible ash fell as far east as the Great Plains (930 miles/1,500 kilometers). More than 500 million tons blew across the United States—the light ash cloud moved across the country in three days and circled the planet in fifteen.[2]

Officials closed airports all around the Pacific Northwest and as far away as North Dakota. Ash is corrosive to machinery and it can also damage crops. Mount St. Helens's arm of destruction reached far and wide.

Hours went by and Dave still had not been found.

Pete Lipman, Dave's mentor and close friend, was among the first to stand on the ridge where Coldwater II had been. It was the next morning: Monday, May 19. Everything was gone—the camping trailer, the beige Ford Pinto wagon Dave had been driving, the trees. Everything. Then Pete dialed the Johnston's phone number in Oak Lawn to convey what they'd found, or rather what they hadn't found—Dave.

When a reporter called Tom Johnston for comment, he said: "It's a million-to-one chance, but we have to clutch it."[3]

Two more days passed and it was apparent to Dave's colleagues that he was deceased. Tom Casadevall had never met Alice and Tom Johnston but they knew of him. He called the family and could tell that the elder Johnston was trying to form a picture in his head. Casadevall felt somebody needed to go see them. They were isolated in Oak Lawn and struggling with the tragedy. Finally, Casadevall said, "Look, I'm going. I am going to fly to Chicago and meet with the Johnstons." He proceeded to do exactly that. He called and relayed his flight information, and Pat and Tom Johnston met him at Chicago's O'Hare Airport.[4]

When they arrived at the Johnston home in Oak Lawn, Alice, Tom, and Pat sat with Casadevall around the kitchen table. He'd brought maps and photos of Mount St. Helens and Coldwater II. Alice asked him the same question repeatedly but in different ways. Her biggest fear was that Dave was incinerated and endured great pain.

Casadevall then explained the theory on how Dave died. Evidence pointed to a compressed wall of air being pushed in front of the debris avalanche, called an air concussion, which is synonymous with air blast or air shock. Casadevall assured Alice that her son didn't suffer. With air shock, death is instantaneous.

Pat would have a recurring nightmare from that day forward. She wondered if her brother might have run inside the trailer and not been killed outright. She thought perhaps USGS had told them the "cleansed version" and she worried her brother may have suffered a much worse death.

Thirty-six years later, Casadevall talked about Dave's death with even more conviction, no doubt strengthened by his later experience working with snow avalanche victims who were killed by air blasts rather than by snow. "Dave would *not* have had time to run inside the trailer. There's a scientific paper that supports the shock wave moved at subsonic speed," he said. "My image is that Dave was outside the trailer, he saw the initiation of the avalanche and reported it by radio, and the shock wave hit within seconds from the start of the blast."

The Johnstons tried to take comfort in Casadevall's presence and his words. They talked of how Dave died doing what he loved. They recalled his last phone call home one week earlier on Mother's Day and how he told his parents that it was a sight very few geologists get to see.

Then with the quiet strength Alice was known for, and with complete exhaustion from not having slept in days, she excused herself and went to her room.

After dinner, Pat and Casadevall took a walk. When they returned, Dave's childhood room was made up for him. Casadevall looked at the posters that still hung on the walls; he was honored to be staying in the room of a man he had admired. As he closed the bedroom door, he discovered a quote by Theodore Roosevelt carefully tacked to the inside:

> It is not the critic who counts; not the man who points out how the strong man stumbles, or where the doer of deeds could have done them better. The credit belongs to the man who is actually in the arena, whose face is marred by dust and sweat and blood; who strives valiantly; who errs, who comes short again and again, because there is no effort without error and shortcoming; but who does actually strive to do the deeds; who knows great enthusiasms, the great devotions; who spends himself in a worthy cause; who at the best knows in the end the triumph of high achievement, and who at the worst, if he fails, at least fails while daring greatly, so that his place shall never be with those cold and timid souls who neither know victory nor defeat.[5]

Dave lived in this childhood bedroom starting at age fifteen. He posted those words as a reminder that no matter the outcome, it is in the striving that we are at our best.

Harry Glicken was overcome with survivor guilt.

"It should have been me," Glicken said over and over. When he learned his mentor and friend was killed, he wept. In the irrational thoughts of the bereaved, Glicken thought his presence with Dave on that ridge might have made a difference. Coldwater II had been "his" post. He felt he had let Dave down.

All accounts say that Glicken pretty much worshipped his mentor. Brugman, who remained close with him after their survival, said, "Harry would have preferred to have placed his life down for Dave."

"That would have been the worst possible scenario," Chris Carlson told Glicken. "Dave would not have wanted it to be you." A colleague agreed: "Dave definitely would have had survivor guilt if he, himself, had lived while his assistant died."

"What happened at Mount St. Helens troubled Harry deeply for a very long time," said Richard Fisher, Glicken's mentor at the University of California–Santa Barbara. "I think it made him even more dedicated than he was before. It certainly reinforced his respect for what volcanoes are capable of."[6]

Glicken dove into the study of Mount St. Helens's debris avalanche like a lifeguard plunges in to save a person from drowning. It was his way to stay afloat in a river of anguish.

Barry Voight returned to the area a few days after the May 18 eruption and headed up the mapping project for the debris avalanche deposit. Glicken worked under Voight, and Voight became one of Glicken's thesis advisors. For the next five years, Glicken tore the debris avalanche apart. He dedicated himself to the study of this hazardous mechanism, and in the process he produced a detailed dissertation that earned him his doctorate in 1986.

Glicken's work helped advance the science of volcanology with Mount St. Helens at the forefront. He added a link to decades of research by Crandell, Mullineaux, and others. Despite the fact that he became a world leader in the study of volcanic debris avalanches, Glicken was unable to fulfill his dream of working for USGS. Budgetary restrictions in the 1980s put a freeze on federal hiring and a cap on USGS staff. This hit him hard, and once again he pushed forward emotionally.

With astute awareness, Glicken had studied the Japanese language—volcanoes in Japan offered many opportunities to research debris avalanches and he found his way there. He did a postdoc with the University of Tokyo and another at the Tokyo Metropolitan University. It was during his time at Tokyo Metropolitan University that another tragedy befell Glicken, one that took his life.

Harry Glicken died eleven years after Dave in a volcanic eruption of Mount Unzen in Japan. He was acting as guide for French volcanologists Katia and Maurice Krafft when the tragedy occurred.

Mount Unzen was in an explosive period and the Kraffts hoped to capture video of a pyroclastic flow, a hazard for which they had little footage.

Harry Glicken, 1981. Photo courtesy of the Glicken family.

"Harry's work at the time was to look at old mudflows," said his sister, Anne. "Sometimes he'd go to a volcano with recent mudflows but his focus was their *history*." Anne said the Kraffts asked her brother to help them out.

To understand why Glicken and the Kraffts were close to Unzen when it erupted, one must review events that led up to that day. In 1982, two thousand people were killed when El Chichón volcano in Mexico erupted and wiped out nine villages. Then in 1985, the village of Armero, Colombia, was nearly obliterated by the eruption of Nevado del Ruiz—23,000 people died.[7] After these tragedies, the worldwide volcanology community vowed that no city would ever again perish due to residents' lack of understanding of the hazards in their backyard. They viewed adequate education about volcanic hazards as something that could help, but educational tools were needed—ones that could be used by various cultures around the world.

Katia and Maurice Krafft specialized in videos of explosive volcanoes in order to contribute to disaster preparedness. It was their video *Understanding Volcanic Hazards* that was used to educate people around Mount Pinatubo (the Philippines) when it began quaking in spring 1991. In a densely populated area, it was imperative that local authorities and citizens grasp the gravity of the situation. Geologists showed the Kraffts' video to the leaders of the Aeta indigenous group who lived on the volcano's flanks. Then, despite their belief that the spirit of the volcano—Apo Mallari—would keep them safe, leaders brought their people down the mountain. Even Philippine president Corazon Aquino is said to have watched the video.

"The Krafft video worked much better than our usual discussions and maps," said Chris Newhall, a geologist with the USGS Volcano Disaster Assistance Program who was at Pinatubo in 1991. "Terms such as ash flows or mudflows meant nothing to folks in an area who had never seen any volcanic activity. The video, especially where it showed damage, was very effective."[8] At least five thousand people evacuated the area totally devastated by the eruption on June 15, 1991.[9] The Kraffts' work helped save them.

Twelve days before Pinatubo erupted, on June 3, 1991, Glicken and the Kraffts were at an observation point near Mount Unzen when it blew. Thirty-nine others were nearby. The trio, along with the thirty-nine, were killed; among them were journalists, police officers, even taxi drivers. The Kraffts died even as their tools were being used to help save lives. Glicken knew the merits of their work and died helping them.

"The Kraffts were dissatisfied with their footage of pyroclastic flows," said Newhall. "That's why they moved in close to Unzen; they were determined to improve their stock of this serious volcanic hazard. They cared deeply for people, especially the poor, who were affected by volcanic eruptions."

Were Glicken and the Kraffts curious to see Unzen's activity? Yes, and you could say that about any volcanologist, albeit from a distance deemed safe. It is also true that these volcanologists were motivated by commitment. Some say Glicken was excited to go; some say he was hesitant. He was likely both, much like Dave at Mount St. Helens, who said he wanted to stay even though he was afraid. In the end, Glicken saw the benefits of accompanying the Kraffts despite the risk.

Survivor guilt is a sticky topic. It can be painful to explore as it brews below the surface.

"Yeah, I got Dave killed," said Doug Lalla in a 2015 interview. Doug's words, made half in jest, came from the fact that he had issued Dave the first invitation to research active volcanoes. "Instead of dead ones," as Doug put it all those years ago.

When questioned about his allusion to guilt, Doug pondered: "Do I feel guilt? Sort of yes, sort of no. The reality is if Dave hadn't gone to Augustine, he'd have gone to Guatemala or somewhere else. On May 18, I woke to my alarm and heard a geologist was missing. It felt like a rock hit me."

Dave certainly may have found his way to active volcanism without Doug. What is important is that Doug opened a door that enabled Dave to accomplish something at Augustine that he viewed as a solid contribution to volcanology— "a link in the chain"—Dave's exact words. Alice Johnston told a reporter about Dave's "link" comment and said, "A parent hangs onto things like that."

Without Dave's experience at Augustine, his instincts and convictions may not have been as strong in 1980—his words in media interviews may have been subdued. But he *had* had the experience—because of Doug.

Often, grief and guilt are inexplicably intertwined. Even Dave's sister Pat succumbed to survivor guilt. For a long time, she didn't realize that's what she was feeling. Psychologists say that guilt after the loss of a sibling is common, but this type of grief tends to be downplayed by society—sympathy flows to parents who lose a child or vice versa—but many don't realize that a sibling forms a part of a person's identity. To lose a sibling with whom you've shared much is to lose a piece of one's self forever. There's guilt about moving on with one's life, reaching new milestones, seemingly "getting over" the loss. Panic can set in as memories begin to dim because it feels as though the loved one slips further away.[10]

There may be others who harbor a measure of guilt among geologists who were monitoring St. Helens in spring 1980 when it erupted. It is common after trauma such as wars, when some go home while others perish, for a question to haunt survivors: *Why me?* This happened after the bombing of the World Trade Center on September 11, 2001. Another day when a blue sky suddenly turned black and debris buried people and property. Two years later, New York City firefighter John Morabito talked with a catch in his throat about six fellow firefighters from Engine Ten who died and how he continued to be riddled with survivor guilt.[11]

Steve Malone expressed his grief this way: "After putting a lot of effort into getting instruments in and trying to get the monitoring going as best we could, I had hope that we would see a change, a progression in activity that would give us forewarning in the hours or days preceding an event that might occur. When that didn't happen, there was a real sense in the lab, for me in particular, that it was for naught. We'd done all this and still we hadn't anticipated the events. People died. Dave died. There was a sense of failure." In the period following May 18, Steve and others who ran the seismic network went through the motions. That didn't change until they saw evidence in the seismic record that another eruption may occur. "We started seeing changes on the order that allowed us to anticipate subsequent eruptions," said Steve. "This sort of dragged us out of despondency."[12]

The seismic network noted a pattern in activity that led to advance warnings of eruptions in July, August, and October 1980. It was a breakthrough that saved further loss of life.

Harry Glicken was nearly on that ridge instead of Dave. Don Swanson would have been in Dave's place if not for a fluke that took him elsewhere on May 17; and Don would have witnessed the eruption from Coldwater II if he had relieved Dave earlier on that Sunday morning.

Don said, "People have asked if Dave may have felt forced into taking Coldwater II that night. Dave was a junior scientist. He may have felt pressure since an older scientist was asking. It's hard for me to answer that question."[13]

Dave agreed to cover Saturday night and if faced with the same situation he would make the same decision. His assistant had been there for two weeks; he was likely relieved to send Harry away at last.

Don Swanson told himself that Dave's death and his unintended role in it was one of those things beyond anyone's control. He told Harry the same thing.

If not for a team of scientists, including Pete Lipman and Steve Malone and Dan Miller and Tom Casadevall and Don Swanson and Harry Glicken and Dave and many others, plus officials who closed areas around Mount St. Helens, thousands might have died. People were evacuated from their mountain homes, and youth camps were empty. Yet many others were in areas that were not cordoned off. Among their stories of survival, there is pain, both physical and emotional.

Venus Dergan and Roald Reitan have such a story. Venus was just nineteen and Roald was twenty in 1980. The young couple made the ninety-mile jaunt from Tacoma to St. Helens on a whim and camped next to the South Fork Toutle River—many miles from the Red Zone—and awoke on May 18 to a deadly mudflow rushing toward their tent. The hot flow grasped and churned them; human specks in a racing river of mud and trees. But they fought their way out and reached safety.[14]

Dave Crockett also escaped death. A reporter for KOMO-TV Seattle, he was driving on a logging road when the ground beneath his car began to crumble. He was forced to walk through hot ash, barely able to breathe or see. He groped his way toward a dot of light at the edge of the black blanket that threatened to smother him; the light grew brighter and he was eventually rescued.[15]

Jim Scymanky, part of a four-man logging crew working overtime hours on a Sunday, was caught in the blast's searing heat and ash and suffered burns on almost half of his body. His tale is one of survival, but his three colleagues died.[16]

The Moore family camped with their two daughters thirteen miles from St. Helens's summit. Their tale of survival also includes death—a couple camped near them was crushed by a tree and killed.[17]

Broken bones, burns, broken hearts, PTSD—these are the stories shared by survivors, harrowing and heartbreaking.

Fifty-seven souls were lost that day. Each with a future that lay in wait and memories of the past within them—these vanished along with their lives.

Some argue that more could have been done. They say logging roads should have been closed to workers, or that the Red and Blue Zones around the summit should have been much larger. The fact remains that the science we have

View from Coldwater II after the eruption; Chris Carlson stares at the volcano that took Dave and fifty-six others. Photo courtesy of Chris Carlson.

today did not exist. Geologists outlined possible hazards they saw at the time, and decision makers concentrated on what was known. Decisions aren't made on conjecture—even when hunches, intuition, or gut feelings turn out to be right.

Mount St. Helens quieted down in mid-April 1980 and those whose livelihoods depended on tourism fought the closures. Many business owners in the area depended (and still depend) on tourism. These businesses mostly scrape by in winter. With spring comes the dollars they need to thrive.

Money should never trump lives, but some felt business figured into decision-making at St. Helens. Fourteen people brought a lawsuit against the state and

Weyerhaeuser Timber for negligence. Among them were families of those who died in the eruption, as well as the lone survivor of the four-man team who sustained burns and other injuries that kept him in intensive rehabilitation for nearly a year. The case against the state was dismissed. The court ruled that decisions were made with information available at the time. Weyerhaeuser settled out of court, a small settlement—half went to lawyers.[18]

Among the fifty-seven who died was Harry R. Truman, who had said, "I'm a part of that mountain and it's a part of me." His statement came to fruition. He *is* a part of the mountain, under the debris avalanche that buried him and his lodge. He couldn't imagine life elsewhere. Truman stayed put, just as he said he would.

Robert Kaseweter and Beverly Wetherald also died in a cabin at Spirit Lake. Kaseweter was a geochemist who volunteered to be a volcano watcher and obtained official permission to be within the Red Zone. He, his fiancée, and his homemade seismometer were buried in the rubble and never found. Kaseweter's sister, Connie, said that since her brother's body was never found, she has sometimes thought of him as still living. But she accepts he is gone, and dwells on a thought, "If he had to die, that's the way, I guess; he loved living on the mountain."[19]

Newlyweds John and Christy Killian were married only seven months when they went camping at Fawn Lake, about nine miles northwest of the summit just beyond Coldwater I (the original USGS observation post). John was twenty-nine; he had a six-year-old son from his first marriage. Besides his love for his child and his new wife, Christy, age twenty, he loved to fish. People think he was in his boat when the volcano burst; Christy was probably still asleep in the tent with their dogs. They were within the Tree Blowdown Zone where a dense forest of giant fir trees were torn from their trunks. John was never found. Christy's skeletal remains were found a year later.[20]

It is important to honor all fifty-seven who died and to be clear about the details. They were *not* daredevils. Most were far from the mountain and believed they were safe. Only three people died within the Red Zone: Harry Truman, Robert Kaseweter, and Beverly Wetherald. The ridge known as Coldwater II where Dave was stationed was not within the Red Zone. It was very close to the boundary line but not inside.[21] In the aftermath of loss, the pain was exacerbated when Governor Dixy Lee Ray erroneously put the blame on the victims. Then President Jimmy Carter followed her lead. After touring the area on May 22, 1980, President Carter held a press conference and stated: "One of the reasons for the loss of life that has occurred is that tourists and other interested people—curious people—refused to comply with the directives issued by the governor, the local sheriff, the state patrol and others, and slipped around highway barricades and entered the area when it was well known to be very dangerous."[22]

Some families of victims heard whispers among neighbors about foolish actions that brought about the deaths of their loved ones. "No one brings their kids to a place they consider unsafe," said Donna Parker, whose brother had been camping nearly three miles outside restricted areas when the volcano erupted.[23]

Barbara Karr lost her husband and two sons in the eruption. Andy was eleven and Mike was nine. She learned of their deaths when a picture hit the newswires of her husband's pickup truck covered with ash, with Andy's lifeless body in the bed of the truck. Barbara didn't question the photographer who took the photo at the time—George Wedding of the *San Jose Mercury*. But a few months later, she requested a meeting with him. She wanted to show Wedding a photo of Andy . . . alive.

Others who perished included local area residents, a geologist working on his PhD, journalists, photographers, a poet/writer, a painter who wanted to capture the mountain's fury on canvas . . . the list goes on. Almost all victims were in places *outside* the Red Zone. A few were doing their jobs, as with Dave, Reid Blackburn, and the loggers. Others volunteered and had permits that endorsed their endeavors.

To understand the details of how a loved one died is important. Perhaps equally important, in the case of the eruption, is that other people hear the truth about what happened. Too many liberties have been taken with the stories of the fifty-seven people who died; too many misrepresentations, dramatizations, and inaccuracies. Each time this happens, it dredges up frustration or hurt for that person's loved ones. This too is part of the aftermath of the eruption—having your loved one's story told in ways that do not do justice to their memory.

DEATH LEAVES A HEARTACHE NO ONE CAN HEAL,
LOVE LEAVES A MEMORY NO ONE CAN STEAL.

From an Irish headstone

11

RECOVERY

DAVE'S BODY WAS NEVER RECOVERED. He is buried in the field, without fanfare—his stated desire.

During a stint as a teaching assistant at the University of Washington, he exclaimed with characteristic enthusiasm, "Just bury me at Newberry Caldera!"*

And to Chris Carlson he had said, "*If* I die young, I hope it's in an eruption." Chris relayed these words to his family in an effort to comfort them in their grief.

Some of Dave's personal effects were retrieved from his hotel in Vancouver and returned to his family. A few months after the eruption, Don Swanson poked around in the area where he thought Dave perished, something he and other USGS folks did with regularity—rain had washed away some of the ash—and he spotted a strap. He dug and found part of a backpack; the name on it was David Johnston.

Meanwhile back at Dave's apartment in Menlo Park, the landlord had expected him to vacate by May 31. With the Johnstons' blessing, Tom Casadevall, Chris Carlson, and Wes Hildreth packed Dave's belongings. The family asked that Dave's clothes be distributed to whomever could use them. Casadevall kept Dave's sport coat. Later, a story about that coat reached Dave's family and it gave them pleasure—it had acquired a life of its own. "We were about the same build,"

---

* A caldera is a steep, bowl-shaped depression formed when a magma chamber empties at a volcano's summit.

said Casadevall. "I wore the sport coat to various talks and events marking the eruption anniversary." In a presentation by fellow colleagues, each one wore it as they took turns at the podium. They dedicated their talks to Dave while wearing his coat—which, by the way, did *not* touch carpet—no one fainted that day.

Newspaper reports named Chris Carlson as Dave's fiancée at the time of his death; however, they weren't formally engaged. "We talked about timelines, but we hadn't formalized it," said Chris. "When someone dies, it puts a period at the end of the sentence. It was left hanging."

Chris flew to Chicago to attend the memorial service held by family. She brought two outfits to wear. The dress Dave liked her in best—bright yellow with a multicolored scarf—and something dark.

"I asked his mom, should I wear what Dave would like or what people expect?" Alice urged her to wear yellow. "That's how I got through that day, wearing something that would make Dave happy. He was a very bright-color person, optimistic.... I didn't want to memorialize something dark... I wanted to honor his sunny disposition."

Chris also brought hundreds of letters with her to Illinois—letters Dave wrote to her over seven years during the times and distances they spent apart. She gave them to Alice without censuring them. They were detailed, wide-ranging, and contained thoughts a young man might not share with his mother; but Chris felt that by sharing them—in their unedited fullness—that it wasn't a violation of Dave's privacy. Rather, they were windows into his life during his twenties when he grew into the man he had become.

Then another letter that Dave had written showed up in his parents' mailbox.

Dave wrote to Ken Gooley's parents after their son's death. He wrote at length about the strong character he saw in their son, and he shared this example: At a high school dance, Ken, Dave, and other boys were clustered, and they saw a girl standing alone. She fell under the juvenile classification of "unpopular kid" and in that moment she clearly felt it. Ken strode over and asked her to dance. This letter, intended to lighten the heavy load after the loss of a son, ended up soothing two sets of parents—the Gooleys mailed it to the Johnstons as a testament to Dave's own character.

It seemed all of Dave's friends shared memories with his family to try to fill the gaps of knowledge about what his life had been like since he left Oak Lawn over a decade earlier. Darrell Herd, who studied at the University of Washington with Dave and was a colleague at USGS–Menlo Park, summed up what he saw: "I'm sure you were able to catch only short glimpses of your son these last several years. Like Dave, I was at UW working on my doctorate in geology.... These last years, I saw the same Dave I knew in graduate school—happy in his work, always enthusiastic, refreshingly positive in what he was doing . . . but it was more, Dave became a rising star in the Geological Survey. His science was nothing less than first-rate. He was a budding world-class volcanologist. I miss him, we all do, he enriched our lives."

Then eleven days after the eruption, President Jimmy Carter penned a letter to Alice and Tom. He expressed his personal gratitude for "David's scientific work in service to the Nation." He also said, "I regard his misfortune as I would the death of a soldier in battle." He closed with: "Rosalynn joins me in prayers for your consolation and in sending you our best wishes."

A highly patriotic Dave would never have dreamed any U.S. president would write to his parents, let alone with regard to him.

In the year after Dave died, personal memorials were held, official ones were erected, pictures poured in from his friends and colleagues, and the media conducted interviews. In the midst of it all, before the first year was up, the Johnstons learned that a movie about the eruption was being made that included a character based on Dave. Producers planned to release it on the first anniversary of the eruption.

"My dad was excited to hear a movie would be made because he wanted people to know about Dave," said Pat. "But my mother wasn't sure."

The family was provided a prescreening of the film. "Unfortunately, my mother's qualms were confirmed. The way it was written is *not* how Dave would want to be portrayed."

Pat compared the movie to *Jaws*: replete with danger vying for precedence over the specter of lost income, and the powers-that-be pitted against the one man who was trying to sound the alarm. In the movie, those powers ranged from the local timber company to politicians; even USGS officials were supposedly part of a cover-up to hide the volcano's lethal potential. The one man sounding the alarm, just as with the sheriff in *Jaws* who wanted to close the beach—you

149

guessed it—the man who fights to close the mountain is supposedly based on David Johnston. Dave did feel that the mountain was dangerous, but he certainly wasn't alone. Many felt as he did.

The Johnston family vehemently objected to the way the movie depicted Dave as hard-charging and at odds with his superiors. The movie showed a senior geologist telling the "Dave" character, "You create chaos wherever you go." In a no-holds-barred statement to the press, Pat said flatly, "That is a lie." *No one* who knew Dave personally or professionally would say that. There were no quarrels between Dave and his superiors. Donal Mullineaux asked him to be cautious in statements to the press. Dave didn't argue with his superiors; that wasn't his way.

Dave's family and friends felt the movie besmirched the reputation of a respectful and conscientious scientist. Steve Malone said, "I got very angry, but learned to take in stride that media sometimes sensationalizes a tidbit of information." Steve was one of a group of scientists who signed a letter protesting the movie. And Zay Smith, the *Chicago Sun-Times* reporter whom Alice helped with his first foray into journalism at fifteen, barraged the movie makers with publicity about the injustice of painting a picture of Dave in such an absurd way.

With Dave's reputation at stake, the Johnston family asked filmmakers to change the character's name under threat of a lawsuit. Alice summed it up succinctly when she told the filmmaker, "We expect you to change the name because we don't expect any more and we expect nothing less." Change it they did. The movie was delayed because the name Johnston was dubbed over with Jackson. So if you watch the movie (against recommendation by anyone who knew Dave), you'll find a main character named Dave *Jackson*—a blond, rebellious, chaos-causing volcanologist who shares nothing with David A. Johnston from Oak Lawn, Illinois, who died in service to his country. He never befriended and drank whiskey with Harry Truman (as depicted in the movie). In fact, Dave was frustrated with Truman's defiance. "He scoffs that nothing will happen and others dismiss the hazards," said the *real* Dave.

Movie producers said they used "dramatic license" to enliven the story.[1] But Dave's loved ones were offended. It is a painful splinter that can never be removed.

Before the movie's release, one other person who lost family at Mount St. Helens called Alice Johnston. Barbara Karr asked Alice one question: "Was there any reference to my kids?" Alice assured her there was none. Then Barbara briefly shared how she had clung to hope that her husband and two sons had survived until she learned of their death from the picture in the newspaper two days later. Alice asked no questions; she listened to Barbara with a heart aching from similar loss. And when she hung up, silent tears streamed.

It is hard to recover when people constantly pick at your pain. This is what happened each time another media outlet exaggerated or bashed Dave's role at Mount St. Helens.

One news article questioned why Dave didn't "follow his own advice." It questioned why he advised others to get off the mountain yet he stayed. The reporter ignored the fact that it was *his job* to advise people of the dangers, and it was *his job* to man the post at Coldwater II the night of May 17.

Another article called him "a volcanologist who once climbed an erupting volcano in Alaska." Clearly, this was written without proper research. Dave did not climb Augustine *as it erupted.* If a volcano erupts, you run away, not up its flanks.

Dave ended up in many books. One said Dave volunteered for the closest observation towers because he was a marathon runner (he was, and a fast one at that) and thought he had a better chance of outrunning an eruption than his older colleagues—a statement that makes him appear full of hubris, which is nonsense.

Nonfiction writers try to get it right. It's challenging and takes enormous chunks of time and research. Still, inaccuracies can make it into black and white. Behind every statement, we look for the intention. Sensationalism, dramatization, exaggeration—these put distance between the truth and as-close-to-the-truth-as-possible.

Those who knew Dave realized that the most meaningful way to honor what he stood for was to continue the work he would be doing alongside them if he had lived.

Harry Glicken wrote to the Johnstons a month after Dave's death. Even as Harry struggled with his own grief, he sought to soothe: "I believe—I know— that continuing the work here is what Dave would like us to do. . . . I'm doing a thesis project on the debris flow which we believe may become the geologic record of the lateral blast, and if so, may bring about a greater realization of the hazards around active volcanoes with similar hummocky deposits. You can be sure that my dissertation will be dedicated to Dave."

This is how the scientists who were at Mount St. Helens dealt with their emotions after the eruption. They worked long and hard hours. Carolyn Driedger said, "That's how we all responded, by working harder and channeling our energy toward problem-solving." That was an excellent coping mechanism according to an expert on survivors of mass violence, Richard Mollica—and the eruption certainly qualified as mass violence—redirection of feelings of powerlessness toward a purposeful activity is therapeutic for trauma and grief. According to Mollica, "Work, work, work. This is the single most important goal of traumatized people."

In the year after the eruption, while Hollywood produced a "dramatically licensed" film, geologists produced something superior in every way—professional papers that summed up their findings of what took place at Mount St. Helens. Their work would change volcanology forever.

Meanwhile, a different kind of recovery was taking place. The area around the volcano was the picture of desolation, and scientists wondered what it would take for the landscape to recover.

Three months after the eruption, ecologists hovered in a helicopter over the barren blast zone and searched for signs of plant or animal life. They were surprised to find a patch of freshly disturbed earth—brown dirt that was brought to the surface by the northern pocket gopher as it burrowed in the ash. Since the gopher lives entirely underground, it was protected from the eruption beneath a mantle of soil.[2]

The following spring, ecologists found prairie lupine—a perennial plant—in full purple bloom. The flower's special root system allows it to grow in the most inhospitable places. And thanks to the dirt unearthed by gophers, lupine found a place to take hold.

As more gophers worked the blast zone, they mixed soil with ash and new plants spread. The lupines colonized the Pumice Plain and population began to boom. Gophers ate the lupine and their numbers increased. With plant life came elk. They too helped spread the interdependent web of life by trampling gopher holes; this created tunnel systems with collapsed entrances that stayed cooler and allowed salamanders to thrive inside them.

Spirit Lake, however, was choked with debris; its oxygen supply was cut off; nothing survived. But as time passed, the debris settled, the water cleared, and sunlight levels rose. Phytoplankton, brought in by birds or wind, began to grow. Phytoplankton are microscopic marine plants that turn sunlight into oxygen—the basic building block of aquatic life. Eventually, the lake began to recover. Amphibians flourished, and when the lake was stocked with fish, they too thrived. Scientists admitted that they had underestimated organisms' ability to disperse. Decades later, downed trees from the blast still float on Spirit Lake's surface; it is shallower, but it is alive—nature's resilience hard at work.

153

The landscape around Mount St. Helens provided a unique opportunity to observe if, how, or when life could return from the dead. In 1982, Congress approved creation of the Mount St. Helens National Volcanic Monument. More than one hundred thousand acres were set aside for research, education, and recreation. A portion of it is designated as a living ecological laboratory. Operated by the Forest Service and the Pacific Northwest Research Station (PNRS), the area's designation as a monument allows geological processes to unfold and lets the ecosystem return to equilibrium on its own. It ensures that all people—the public and scientists alike—are able to observe the remarkable recovery.

Ecologist Charlie Crisafulli of PNRS began research at St. Helens within weeks after the May 18 eruption; his work spans decades. In response to a visitor's comment at a viewpoint along Spirit Lake Highway that grumbled about the amount of land cordoned off from the public, Crisafulli clarified—no areas are cut off from the public except the crater. There are, however, constraints in certain areas where public are asked to stick to the trails—these areas represent 2 percent of the blast area. For example, hikers are asked to stick to the trail that bisects the Pumice Plain—one of the most devastated areas around the summit where vegetation has been slow to return.

Those who grew up around St. Helens remember when they could roam as free as the elk, but there are still ample opportunities to climb, hike, and explore. Each year, thousands climb to the mountain's summit. The annual Mother's Day climb is popular; men and women flock to the volcano flaunting dresses, tutus, and colorful headwear. Some hold handmade signs that say, "I love you, Mom." This image conjures some of Dave's last words.

It took twenty years for some to turn the corner on recovery. A ceremony marking the twentieth anniversary of the eruption brought people together from surrounding communities, people who had lost loved ones or suffered injuries. There had been so much emphasis on the landscape, the cleanup, and the science, that it seemed, to some, that the dead had been swept away with the ash.

In 2000, when Cowlitz County commissioners placed a plaque with fifty-seven names among a grove of trees, it was a moment of healing.

Held at the Hoffstadt Bluffs Visitor Center with a view of the upper Toutle Valley and Mount St. Helens, the ceremony was kicked off by a Boy Scout color guard. There's no record of how many of the fifty-seven were former scouts.[3] We know there was at least one.

Three hundred people gathered to honor those who died during or because of the eruption. Carolyn Driedger was among the attendees.

"Looking back, I know I had PTSD," said Carolyn. "It was too hard to go back after the eruption. Thinking of the loss of human life and seeing the transformation of a once beautiful landscape, I had zero attraction. It wasn't until the twentieth anniversary ceremony where dignitaries honored everyone involved that I began to feel better. I guess you could say that the words I heard at the ceremony helped me to move on. I *really* wanted to move on."

Don Swanson also attended a twentieth anniversary gathering, but at the Johnston Ridge Observatory. Don's thoughts turned to the idea that it could have been Dave standing in his place, attending an event on a ridge named after Don.

Healing after the loss of a loved one is never complete—the world becomes forever bifurcated. There is "before," when the person still walked the earth, and there is "after," when he or she walks no more. Alice, Tom, and Pat Johnston did their best to heal, or at least give the semblance of it.

Alice told an interviewer, "Life isn't a destination, life is a journey, and David had thirty years of a good journey." Privately, she and Tom mourned the loss of a second child, and naturally, some regrets surfaced. Alice wished they hadn't started him in school as the youngest. She also wished she hadn't given away his dogs. She would have read Dave's diary, the one in which he expressed feelings never uttered aloud.

Memorial grove and plaque at Hoffstadt Bluffs. Photo courtesy of Cowlitz County.

Tom spoke of regret also. He met with Seattle journalist Jeff Renner a month after Dave died and said, "I miss him a lot, and part of me wishes I never encouraged his interest in geology and volcanoes. But I couldn't do that. He loved his work and used to say that each day was an adventure, an opportunity to learn something new, to use that knowledge to be a better scientist and to help other people."[4] While reporting on events at St. Helens, Renner had grown to like and respect Dave. He had put several media interviews of Dave onto a VHS tape and gave it to Tom.

Pat also felt regret as she analyzed every word of her last conversations with her brother. Words said in jest remained suspended in midair. Their way was to kid each other; neither knew there wouldn't be time for other more sentimental moments.

Psychologists call regret the most haunting form of distress. Alternative actions, the what-ifs, are easy to imagine. We know a measure of regret is part of life; however, not all regrets fall into the same category. Bronnie Ware researched the top regrets of the dying and number one was: "I wish I'd had the courage to live a life true to myself."[5] For Dave, a career as a volcanologist was his way of staying true to his passion. His family gripped tightly to this idea as life went on without him.

Alice survived Dave by twenty-five years. In that time, she became a grandmother and gained a son-in-law. She continued her job at the General Services Administration, then finished out her career at the National Archives.

Tom survived his son by twenty-nine years. He became a grandfather and spoiled his grandkids to the extent that Alice was compelled to gently intervene from time to time. After Tom retired, he hung around Pat's home; tinkering and fixing anything that was broken. In truth, the handyman role gave him reason to spend more time around her and her kids. Tom often made up wild, boisterous stories for his grandkids. But when he spoke to them about the uncle they never met, he focused on character not deeds.

Born one of three, Pat has been an only child since she was twenty-seven years old. The brother she used to call "Evil David" had turned into a best friend who brought her to her first concert—the Rolling Stones at the University of Illinois. As is her way, Pat jokes, "I just started to like him then I lost him." To be fair, he kept a picture of an orangutan in his college dorm room that he referred to as his sister. But the wallet recovered after he died held a real one of Pat, a beautiful one.

When Dave performed dangerous fieldwork, he trusted his sister with his stories. Sometimes he expressed fear and she worried. One letter in particular was unsettling. Before he left on a trip to Augustine, he wrote Pat and said, "If I die" and ended with a last will of sorts. He asked her to commit it to memory then burn it, which she did.

Chris Carlson said, "As Pat's life continued to build, Dave would have been so proud to be her audience." Dave also would have been a proud uncle to her kids. His namesake—first name David, middle name Johnston—resembles his uncle with blond hair, a full beard, and a ready smile. Now older than his uncle was when he died, David recalls how his grandma Alice liked to buy books for her grandkids—one of the last gifts he received from his grandma was a copy of *Writer's Market*—a crucial tool for writers breaking into the business. "My grandma encouraged writing in me," he said. David attended his uncle's alma mater, the University of Illinois, and majored in English. After college, he sold a comedy/satire play to a small Chicago theater; the play garnered good reviews. He later moved on to other endeavors with a steadier paycheck, including teaching.

Pat's second child is a son, Mark, whose baby pictures resemble those of his uncle. Mark also shares the same rare gene mutation that results in a full head of blond hair and a beard that grows in red. Perhaps out of compassion, or perhaps to allay his mom's persistent fears, he told her that he thought she'd prepared him for the world.

While all parents try to educate their kids about situations they may confront in the future, *preparation* has been a central theme for Pat and her kids. Like her brother, she was a product of the 1960s and remembers duck-and-cover drills, sonic booms, and the deadly tornado that killed a girl from her high school. She understands the harsh reality of losing an uncle (Artie) who was snatched by nature's fury and a newborn sister who didn't come home from the hospital. A series of traumatic experiences led to feelings of vulnerability, and eventually hypervigilance set in. Storms at sea, storms in your hometown, storms that burst forth from the ground: they left a distinct imprint. When her son David talked of flying on the day he would turn thirty years and five months old—the exact age her brother was when he died—Pat asked him not to fly—*not on that day.* Alice shared Pat's fear of the unknown; Alice revealed hints of her deep-seated trepidation when a tornado threatened Oak Lawn in the 1990s and she said, "This time, I thought it was going to take us."

Pat's youngest child also mirrors the Johnston side. Molly has vibrant red hair like her Grandpa Tom and a keen sense of humor. After completing her degree (also at University of Illinois), she pursued comedic performance; but unlike her uncle she can perform without fainting.

Two other kids became part of Pat's family when she and her husband took in two teenage boys who had tragically lost their parents. Pat called her mom, crying, when she found out about the boys' plight. Alice urged her toward the thought Pat and her husband already had—to take them in. (Alice had turned down an offer from a friend's family when she was fifteen and needed to get away from home; she contemplated that decision later in life.) Pat's son David said of the family additions, "It made my parents happy taking care of them."

All five kids are now grown.

Pat spent her career as a physical therapist, ministering to the aches of others. As a daughter, she watched out for both parents when their health failed. Her sense of humor is engaging; you can't help but laugh at her description of Christmas 1979 (Dave's last one): "He was home and couldn't wait for me to wake up Christmas morning, and like a kid, he repeatedly walked down the hall past my bedroom door and each time he sort of fell into it." He succeeded in waking her up so they could open presents. The ribbons and bows he untied revealed . . . leisure suits. "The light blue one with dark stitching was hideous," said Pat. And as she recalls these memories, she giggles; she's a sister again.

Poet Linda Ellis wrote about the dash printed between the years of a person's birth and death. Dave's dash consisted of thirty years and five months. Where the dash leaves off, legacy begins.

His legacy is intertwined with a beautiful mountain that turned violent and reminded people that America does indeed need to pay attention to its volcanoes.

Beyond the destruction wrought by Mount St. Helens is its own legacy; one filled with critical lessons and continued creation.

LEGACY . . . IT'S PLANTING SEEDS IN A GARDEN
YOU NEVER GET TO SEE.

Hamilton: An American Musical

PART FOUR

LEGACY TAKES
MANY FORMS

IF I HAVE SEEN FURTHER THAN OTHERS,
IT IS BY STANDING UPON THE SHOULDERS OF GIANTS.

Isaac Newton

12

VOLCANOLOGY'S GIANT LEAP

THE STUDY OF VOLCANOLOGY IN AMERICA began with a revolution. Far from the mainland, an armed insurrection led by American businessmen overthrew rulers who had reigned over a chain of islands in the Northern Pacific—islands with fertile soil, which drew planters and merchants. Such was the fall of the last Hawaiian monarchy in 1892—the queen was removed by force, and the businessmen, with the help of American troops, installed an interim government.[1] Then in 1899, the United States annexed the islands, which set the stage for America's first volcano observatory.

Thomas Jagger, a geology professor from the Massachusetts Institute of Technology (MIT), had a grand vision. Jagger witnessed the deadly aftermath of volcanic eruptions during his explorations, and one in particular deeply disturbed him—29,000 people died when Mount Pelée erupted on the Caribbean Island of Martinique in 1902. Jagger wanted to open observatories around the world in order to protect life and property based on scientific knowledge, and he wanted to start in Hawaii. As he set about raising funds to open an observatory, he found Lorrin Thurston—the same man who led the insurrection against the monarchy years earlier. Thurston formed the Hawaiian Volcano Research Association and pledged support. So with funds from Thurston's group, as well as from MIT, Thomas Jagger opened the Hawaiian Volcano Observatory (HVO) in 1912. This private funding arrangement kept the HVO afloat until 1919 when the U.S. government took over.

American funds for volcanology research in the twentieth century took a back seat to other national priorities, and control of the HVO bounced around. Initially, the Weather Bureau took over when private funding ended. Then the Geological Survey took control; then the National Park Service managed it in the years building up to and through World War II. Finally in 1948, the Geological Survey became the permanent administrator of the HVO. It was just in time. Mauna Loa, Hawaii's largest volcano—and the world's largest active volcano— was about to erupt.

Mauna Loa, located on Hawaii's big island, entered an eruptive stage in 1949 that lasted through 1950. During one eruption, rivers of lava cut a major highway in three places. USGS needed more staff and equipment; so it was that Mauna Loa led to a growth spurt for America's Volcano Hazards Program (VHP)—the umbrella under which volcano projects were housed. USGS received much-needed funding that enabled them not only to increase research in Hawaii but also to initiate volcanic hazard research projects in the Cascade Range. Although the HVO continued to dominate VHP funds, work in the Cascades during the 1950s and 1960s attracted scientists such as Rocky Crandell and Donal Mullineaux.

Even though the theory of continental drift was generally accepted, many question marks hovered over scientists' heads. Then Canadian geologist J. Tuzo Wilson had an idea, which some say came to him in a dream . . . about a mythical goddess.

While Pliny the Younger's carefully recorded reports of Mount Vesuvius's ashfall, noxious vapors, and "storm of stones" were crucial to scientists, Wilson used *oral* stories to put another geological footprint in the sands of time. Wilson heard of the goddess Pele, whom Polynesians said had done some strategic island-hopping. They talked of her journey that started with the northernmost Hawaiian island of Niihau and ended with the southernmost island—the big island of Hawaii. Each time Pele landed on an island, a volcano began to spark and burn; and on the islands she left behind, once-active volcanoes fizzled and went dormant. Wilson envisioned a geological explanation for Pele's fiery "journey"—one that explained why active volcanism seemed to disappear, only to spring up elsewhere. He thought the stories suggested that the goddess was actually a stationary "hot spot" in the earth's crust that allowed magma to rise upward through the seafloor, and as the oceanic tectonic plate moved over the hotspot, island after island was formed.[2]

Leading geophysics journals told Wilson that he was indeed dreaming; they rejected his theory. Instead, his article "A Possible Origin of the Hawaiian Islands" was published by a small Canadian physics magazine in March 1963. Then the U.S. military, which had helped scientists understand the theory of continental drift through its network of sensors, made testing of Wilson's theory possible— he was eventually vindicated. We now call Wilson's dream-idea plume theory, which explains why volcanoes exist far away from the boundaries of tectonic plates.

Despite America's work in volcanic hazards research, Congress didn't formalize a budget line for VHP until 1968. The following year, Crandell submitted a request for funds to study volcanic hazards in the Cascades, including Mount St. Helens.[3] Together with Mullineaux, the geologists wrote a sort of biography of Mount St. Helens—the now infamous 1978 Geological Survey Bulletin 1383-C—with its equally infamous forecast based on the past. They referred to St. Helens as "an especially dangerous volcano" and wrote that an eruption was likely in the not-too-distant future.

Despite many important research projects, volcanology's giant leap came with the eruption of Mount St. Helens on May 18, 1980. Geologists had no historical basis to anticipate the magnitude of events that eventually unfolded on that fateful May day.

In 2015, Tom Casadevall said, "We've had thirty-five years to study the 1980 eruption. We knew there was an earthquake, landslide, and directed blast. Initially, we didn't know exactly how they were related."

Casadevall continued, "There was a lot of groundwater in the volcano, and as gases came up from the depth, they were absorbed into that water. Within the volcano, there were several springs and they came out on its surface. Also, it was completely covered with ice sheets. All that water saturated the volcano and this is why we didn't get the gas levels we thought we'd see."

The mountain didn't behave as expected, but erupt it did, and geologists went back into the field as soon as possible and worked knee-deep in hot ash. They needed to know the mechanisms that snuffed out fifty-seven lives and could have taken thousands. A year and a half later, one hundred thirty scientists produced USGS Professional Paper 1250, "The 1980 Eruptions of Mount St. Helens, Washington," which they dedicated to David Johnston. Dave's colleagues included his work at St. Helens and named him co-author on four papers—all having to do with gas studies that began in March 1980 when the volcano first stirred. At 844 pages and seven and a half pounds, Professional Paper 1250 was like a new life—it breathed knowledge into multiple areas of volcanology—and its words gave testimony to what happened that day and in the eruptions that followed later that year.[4]

The eruption on May 18 was the main event, but other smaller ones followed on May 25, June 12, July 22, August 7, and October 16–18. In fact, 1980 marked the beginning of an eruptive stage that lasted six years, and scientists were there to observe, record, and report. They also were there to warn of subsequent eruptions. Geologists announced in *Science* magazine that "thirteen eruptions of Mount St. Helens between June 1980 and December 1982 were predicted tens of minutes to, more generally, a few hours in advance. The last seven of these eruptions, starting with that of mid-April 1981, were predicted between three days and three weeks in advance. Precursory seismicity, deformation of the crater floor and the lava dome, and to a lesser extent gas emissions provided telltale evidence of forthcoming eruptions."[5]

In addition, research at St. Helens enabled scientists to define and identify the directed blast mechanism. Other volcanoes were re-examined, including Bezymianny, the Russian volcano that Dave and others referred to in the weeks before the eruption.

Mount St. Helens's continued activity crystallized the need for constant monitoring of the Cascade volcanoes. USGS required an observatory in the area, along with sufficient resources, and a coordinated communications network so that hazards could be quickly conveyed to government and emergency responders. After discussion at the highest levels, a volcano observatory was established in the Cascades—dedicated to the one USGS member ever to have perished in a volcanic eruption.

The Cascades Volcano Observatory (CVO) in Vancouver, Washington, was dedicated in Dave's honor. A second observatory in the United States was indeed a pivotal step for volcanology—the CVO's location enabled scientists to research active volcanism in unprecedented ways.

A dedication ceremony was held in 1982, and Alice, Tom, and Pat Johnston flew to Vancouver to attend. After receiving enough condolence letters to fill up multiple large red three-ring binders, Alice prepared a speech intended to convey their family's gratitude to those who shared stories about the young man who left home at seventeen with big ambitions and met a devastating demise. Following are the words Alice spoke:

> Thank you on behalf of the Johnston family for the one thousand acts of kindness and thoughtfulness you've shown us. Your beautiful letters illuminated David's life for us.... David was at UW's seismic station when it became certain that St. Helens was alive and striving. David was so excited, he danced with Steve Malone's wife down the hall. He was immensely enthusiastic about the chance to study this change, to learn the forces involved, and to try to read the signs and signals.
>
> He shared your goal–to develop reliable ways to predict volcano behavior to safeguard the people who are in danger when the mountains move. He was tremendously proud to be here with you, as part of this team. He was challenged here. He was fulfilled here. He loved it here. And he is here forever now. And by giving this building his name, you are making sure that his part in your work didn't end at 8:32 that morning in 1980. You are keeping him with you, as part of this team.

After Mount St. Helens's eruption, VHP experienced additional critical growth spurts. Besides establishment of the CVO, three other observatories were eventually opened—in Alaska, in California, and a virtual observatory called the Yellowstone Volcano Observatory (a consortium of eight organizations). USGS already had branch offices in California where Dave worked and in Alaska where he was to move in June 1980; formalizing operations in these places allowed the Geological Survey to operate at a higher level of efficiency.

Even as observatories opened in the United States, volcanic tragedies continued around the world. In 1982, two thousand people died when El Chichón volcano erupted in Mexico.[6] Then in 1985, Nevado del Ruiz volcano killed twenty-three thousand. The concept of a worldwide team to assess volcano hazards had entered embryonic stage in 1980—the groundwork was laid by the expertise and experience learned at Mount St. Helens, and the USGS had begun collaborating with other countries—Nevado del Ruiz made it clear that a formal program was needed. Thus an international volcanic rapid response team was created—administered by USAID's Office of Foreign Disaster Assistance and USGS—called the Volcano Disaster Assistance Program, or VDAP (pronounced VEE-dap).

With 1,500 potentially active volcanoes worldwide, VDAP was set up to respond to those who request assistance—either in-country or remotely. VDAP influence can be found around the world; staff help to assess, prepare for, and respond to volcano emergencies.

America and its territories have more active volcanoes than any country except Indonesia. Apart from the intrinsic rewards of helping fellow global citizens, VDAP has an important domestic return; collaboration with international scientists improves America's capabilities to understand and advance risk-mitigation strategies. Lessons learned elsewhere are applicable to 169 active volcanoes monitored by USGS, most of which are located in Alaska, Hawaii, and the western United States. And of the eighteen volcanoes identified by USGS as "very high threat," ten are in the Cascades—and Mount St. Helens is the most active.[7]

Scientists marked the tenth anniversary of Mount St. Helens' eruption with a symposium on May 18, 1990. It was a chance to review the lessons that had emerged from the destruction, and many of the scientists who worked during the aftermath presented research papers.

Harry Glicken wrote: "Mount St. Helens provided the first opportunity to correlate visual observations, photo documentation, and stratigraphic studies of resultant avalanche deposits." The correlation of these was documented by Glicken and others and led to improved understanding of the mechanism that became recognized as a common process at volcanoes—the rockslide–debris avalanche.[8]

Mindy Brugman reported on the interaction between glaciers and the eruption. All thirteen of the glaciers that covered the mountain in 1980 thawed and the meltwater contributed to torrential floods and devastation.[9]

And Dan Miller spoke about the American segment of the Cascade Range and its average of two eruptions per century over the past several thousand years.

Overall, the symposium stressed the importance of volcanic hazard assessments for mitigating risk for the public. But as the 1990s dawned, so began another deadly decade—for volcanologists—and the entire profession paused and asked the question, *How do we balance potential scientific rewards with the risks we take in doing what we do?*

Volcanologists are certainly aware and accept that certain dangers come with the job; however, mitigating personal risk was a topic they wanted to discuss in the face of continued loss of colleagues. Harry Glicken and the Kraffts died in 1991. Then in 1993, eight volcanologists were killed and others were severely injured in just two incidents. Six were killed during a field trip to the summit of Galeras volcano in Colombia in January 1993*—the excursion was part of a United Nations workshop titled International Decade for Natural Disaster Reduction. Then just two months after Galeras, two more volcanologists were killed at the crater rim of a volcano in Ecuador.

Don Swanson spoke about the back-to-back tragedies:

> Let us praise the curious as we mourn the dead. . . . I am disheartened by the recent deaths of volcanologists in the field but encouraged by the general understanding that the volcanological community has shown. No one wants the death rate to continue unchecked, but no one is seriously suggesting cutting back on field observations by volcanologists either. The best way to reduce fatalities is to understand the volcano better. . . . It is well to remember that volcanology is the study of volcanoes, and purely scientific curiosity-driven motives are as justified as those designed purely to mitigate risks. . . . Curiosity leads to understanding, and understanding is the paramount goal of the science, as well as the soundest basis for reducing risk. Volcanologists who are curious will get themselves into trouble and sometimes die because of it. It is often stated that we must weigh the potential benefits and risks before doing something perceived as risky. Of course we must, but it is mathematically impossible to solve one equation with two unknowns, and generally the potential benefits and risks are both unknowns.[10]

A 1996 paper attempted to identify some of the "unknowns"—the factors that determined death or survival among the group that went to Galeras's summit.[11] The goal of the investigation was to improve the future safety of

---

* Three tourists were also killed when Galeras erupted; the ensuing report on Galeras discourages tourism near active volcanoes.

people—scientists and tourists alike—who might visit an active volcano. Peter Baxter and Austin Gresham of the University of Cambridge wrote: "More volcanologists are working on active volcanoes than ever before, and since 1979, fifteen have been killed by eruptions." That average of almost one per year put volcanology under a microscope—the science was growing and its practitioners' safety needed to be part of the maturation process.

Baxter and Gresham reported on lessons from Galeras and recommended best practices for fieldwork. This included: heat-resistant and water-resistant coveralls and hard hats; constant radio communication with the local volcano observatory; a planned means of rescue in case of an incident; a plan to leave crater areas well before nightfall or upon indication of impending cloud cover, both of which can impede or prevent rescue; and minimizing the number of scientists to those absolutely necessary. Dave did this when he sent Carolyn Driedger and Mindy Brugman back to Vancouver on May 17, 1980; he stressed that only one person was needed on the ridge that night.

The array of personal risks taken at Mount St. Helens in 1980 is different than those taken decades later—scientists have learned much. It was heartening to hear a geologist with VDAP say in 2016, "Since we lost Dave Johnston in 1980, the USGS and VDAP have lost no one to volcano incidents; nor has VDAP had any serious injuries."[12] USGS attributes this record to their staff being safety conscious around active volcanoes. Still, all volcanologists deserve to be safe, including those outside USGS. It is up to each scientist who works on volcanoes, as well as those who lead others during fieldwork, to ensure that safety protocols are strictly observed.

Dave's colleagues began calling the location where he died "Johnston Ridge" soon after the eruption. Seventeen years later, a visitor and learning center opened on the ridge that affords a direct view into the volcano's crater and of the blast zone. It is named the Johnston Ridge Observatory (JRO). Those who work and volunteer at the site know how important it is that no one forget what happened there. It is much more than a place that highlights history; it is a living laboratory where active volcanism continues.

An extension of Route 504 had to be built specifically to reach the JRO. No one except geologists had dug in the area for over a decade. Then during construction of the road in 1993, workers found parts of the trailer from Coldwater II.

Media had a heyday. Richard Waitt wrote to Dave's parents right away: "Four of us from the CVO were at Johnston Ridge where three days earlier roadbuilders unearthed a few remains of the USGS trailer, which we had also unearthed and reburied years ago. Nothing personal of Dave's was there; broken trailer parts, some plastic cups. All of us who knew Dave still feel the strong sense of loss whenever we get near that site."

Dave's family came to the area once again when the JRO was dedicated in 1997. They watched the documentary that airs in its auditorium, which includes an actor's voice shouting Dave's last radio transmission as he saw the blast begin— "This is it!" Those words, even spoken by an actor, are soul-searing to hear.

"Other than Oak Lawn, I feel closer to Mount St. Helens than any other place in the world because I know David's there," said Tom Johnston after the dedication ceremony.

Years later, Pat returned to the JRO with a friend. She avoided local pit stops along the way because she didn't want to come across a piece of the trailer or any other item that might have belonged to her brother. Standing at the ridge, Pat kept her distance from tourists. A private person, a private pain; she didn't want to share her story. Only her friend and a park ranger knew she was there that day.

One thousand nine hundred and one years before Mount St. Helens erupted, Pliny the Younger chronicled what he saw after Mount Vesuvius erupted, but the science hadn't advanced *enough* between those two eruptions in 79 AD and 1980 to forecast the events that took place on May 18 at Mount St. Helens. Many crucial scientific reports were issued before Mount St. Helens erupted, but it was *after* Mount St. Helens became the most-studied volcano in history that volcanology grew exponentially—advancements made possible because of those who meticulously documented and published important lessons.

Science depends on its literature—sharing findings leads others toward greater understanding—as with the two eloquent letters penned by Pliny and the reams of reports that have spewed forth from countless other scientists. Dave published as much as he could in the time he had.

The list of papers and articles attributed to Dave would be smaller if not for those who gave him credit for work he performed before his death. His paper on the eruptive mechanisms of Alaska's Augustine volcano was part of his 1978 dissertation, but he was working on other pieces about Augustine before he died. Among Dave's personal belongings retrieved from his apartment in Menlo Park were drafts of papers on his work.

Several years later, Richard Waitt, who by then worked at the CVO, wrote to Alice and Tom Johnston to tell them that Dave's drafts would be used for a professional paper on Augustine, and that Dave would be listed as second coauthor, ahead of Waitt's own name. The idea for the paper began when Hiroki Kamata of the Geological Survey of Japan was a visiting scientist at the CVO and read a detailed retrospective about the geologist for whom the CVO was named. Kamata was so impressed by Dave's PhD thesis on Augustine that he planned a geological mapping project at Augustine in 1988. Together with Richard Waitt, Kamata re-examined the 1976 deposits Dave had written about. Kamata and Waitt wrote, "The 1976 eruption sequence and deposits were documented in Johnston's thesis. . . . Our field study was built on his thesis and his unpublished material, including rough-draft manuscripts on file at the USGS in Anchorage."

In spring 1991, the international, peer-reviewed *Bulletin of Volcanology* included, "Stratigraphy, Chronology, and Character of the 1976 Pyroclastic Eruption of Augustine Volcano, Alaska," by Hiroki Kamata, David A. Johnston, and Richard B. Waitt. It was an honorable thing to do, not only to give credit to Dave for his work but to write his parents and tell them. It showed Alice and Tom more footprints left by their son.

The article Dave submitted to *Science* magazine before he died was published posthumously on July 25, 1980—"Volcanic Contributions of Chlorine to the Stratosphere: More Significant Than Previously Estimated?" In it, Dave stated that more research was needed in order to understand volcanic chlorine emissions. And his chlorine work has helped inform that research. The chemical industry argued that volcanoes may control the stratospheric chlorine budget; however, NASA research indicates that "removal of chlorine from eruption columns arises because volcanic plumes contain roughly 1,000 times more water than chlorine. The water condenses as the plume lofts and cools, and chlorine is readily scavenged by liquid water."[13] NASA makes it clear—ozone depletion is caused primarily by manmade compounds that contain chlorine. As skeptics such as Ian Plimer (an Australian geologist, author, and one of the world's notable climate change deniers)[14] debate natural versus anthropogenic activities that impact the earth, Dave's article continues to be cited into the twenty-first century—when the words "volcanoes, chlorine, and stratosphere" are used in an internet search, third on the results list is Dave's article.[*]

Then in 1981, another publication came out to which Dave had contributed—a 189-page field guide to volcanic terranes in Washington, Idaho, Oregon, and Northern California.[15] Julie Donnelly-Nolan wrote: "We owe special posthumous thanks to Dave Johnston for conceiving the field trip ideas, overseeing the planning and arrangements for the trips, and maintaining his sense of humor in spite of the last-minute airline strike, and reminding us gently but firmly to produce the promised articles." Wes Hildreth contributed an in-depth retrospective about Dave's life for the field guide, the same one that piqued Hiroki Kamata's interest in Dave's work at Augustine.

Included in the 844-page tome on Mount St. Helens released in 1981 were the four papers coauthored by Dave; it states that since March 1980 when the volcano became active once more, the study of gas emissions has been "an integral part of USGS monitoring programs." Dave was hired by USGS to expand this type of research in the Cascades and Alaska; after he died, other scientists grabbed the baton and have been running ever since—they can be found in laboratories and observing volcanoes around the world.

Based on a letter from *National Geographic* dated April 16, 1980, Dave sent a proposal for an article on volcanoes in early 1979. The science editor was still interested after a year's time and asked Dave to call him upon his return from St. Helens. Dave had hoped to work for *National Geographic* back when he was pursuing photojournalism—his article would have been the merging of dreams.

Harry Glicken also contributed important literature before his death. His dissertation project on Mount St. Helens's debris avalanche influenced studies worldwide. Suddenly, geologists recognized debris avalanches at numerous volcanoes around the globe based on criteria defined by Harry. He was named author of a paper, published posthumously, with detailed geologic maps that illustrate associations between Mount St. Helens's landslide/debris avalanche, directed blast, and destructive lahars.[16]

Harry was also honored with the dedication of a memorial issue of the *Journal of Volcanology and Geothermal Research* (*JVGR*) in 1995. He had begun assembling research papers on modeling with Yoshiaki Ida. After Harry died, Barry

---

[*] Dave's 1980 *Science* article was cited eighty-one times by mid-2016; that number increased to ninety-one times by mid-2018.

Voight stepped in to assist Ida and together they coordinated the memorial issue. Word went out and Harry's colleagues responded; so many papers flowed
in that some had to be printed in other issues of *JVGR*. A poem was included in
the memorial issue called "Remembering Harry," written by Peter Frenzen. It
describes Harry as assembling pieces of the mountain . . . "so others might see
its hidden fury."

Standing on the shoulders of giants is how we see higher and farther. All giants
start somewhere. They learned and grew and stumbled and got up and kept

going. Some, such as Dave Johnston and Harry Glicken and Rocky Crandell
are gone, but it is work done by them and countless others that enables current
practitioners to add further links in the chain of knowledge.

THE MORE YOU KNOW ABOUT THE PAST,
THE BETTER PREPARED YOU ARE FOR THE FUTURE.

Theodore Roosevelt

TWENTY-FIRST CENTURY
AND BEYOND

A QUARTER-OF-A-MILLION DOLLARS has been awarded in Dave's name to fund the education of future scientists. The David A. Johnston Memorial Award for Research Excellence is administered by the University of Washington's Department of Earth and Space Sciences.

Lee Fairchild, who was with Dave at Mount St. Augustine the summer of 1977, was a University of Washington grad student when Dave died. Lee was also Dave's friend and former classmate; he spearheaded the fellowship that still exists in Dave's name.

Lee, Steve Malone, and others planned a special presentation in late 1980 to raise money to establish the fund. Announcements for the presentation went out, and one thousand people showed up and filled the university's largest lecture hall to capacity. By the first anniversary of Dave's death, thirty thousand dollars had been raised and the first two fellowships were awarded. Thirty-eight years later, almost ninety students have received the fellowship—granted to students in geology and geophysics.

"Built into the guidelines for the fellowship is something Dave and I firmly believed in," said Lee, "that geology and geophysics need equal emphasis. I wrote up what the fellowship would look like and how it would be administered. At the time, the two departments didn't talk to each other. The fellowship was set up in a way that *forced* them to talk; it linked them together."[1]

Steve Malone said, "When the fellowship was established, there were separate grad programs for geology and geophysics and there was some rivalry between the two, but that's all gone; they now fall under one department."

Asked whether Lee thought the fellowship's structure might have influenced the confluence of the two disciplines, he answered, "Whether it had an influence, I can't say. That was the hidden agenda; it is what was desired by Dave and me."

The funds support science that girdles the world—from research in New Zealand to water quality and mineral analyses in Greenland. Recipients say that the funds have enabled them to perform experiments that would otherwise have been impossible.

Lee sat on the fellowship committee until 1984, when he graduated from the University of Washington and left the area. Years later, he is one of the stewards of the fund. Lee summed it up nicely when he wrote in 1981: "Through this scholarship it is hoped that David's remarkable energy and creativity will be remembered forever and passed down to future geoscientists." To be sure, part of Lee, Steve, and others are woven into this award program—it is part of their legacy also.

More than one fellowship exists to honor a geologist who died on May 18, 1980. Thirty-two-year-old James F. Fitzgerald Jr. was pursuing his doctorate and was engaged in fieldwork in the Mount St. Helens area when it erupted.

On the night of May 17, Fitzgerald camped in his car about seven miles west-northwest of the volcano while his companions, Barry Johnston (no relation to Dave) and his wife, Trixie Anders, chose to stay in a motel. Barry and Trixie escaped death because Barry insisted on a big breakfast before a long day of volcano watching. If they hadn't stopped, they would have perished along with their friend.[2] Fitzgerald was at Spud Mountain when heavy ashfall reached him; rescuers found him in his Datsun, asphyxiated.

Fitzgerald was attending the University of Idaho when he died; however, his undergrad in geology was from the University of Akron. For this reason, his family and friends chose the University of Akron to establish a scholarship that honors his memory. The James F. Fitzgerald Jr. Memorial Scholarship was established in 1980. It is awarded to an outstanding senior in the Department of Geology each year.

Fellowships and other educational opportunities can advance scientific knowledge. This was also the goal in building the Johnston Ridge Observatory, as well as the Science and Learning Center at Coldwater, which opened in 1993. Supported by the Forest Service and the Mount St. Helens Institute (MSHI), the Coldwater center helps MSHI reach one hundred thousand adults and children annually with hiking and climbing adventures as well as volunteer and stewardship work.

These visitor and learning centers elucidate the fact that volcanoes have positive aspects. Gaseous emissions from volcanic vents formed the earth's earliest oceans and atmosphere over billions of years—vital ingredients that allowed life such as plants and people to evolve. Eighty percent of the earth's surface is of volcanic origin—above and below sea level—and some of the most fertile soils come from broken down volcanic materials. These soils produce food and have fostered civilizations throughout history.

Also, geothermal energy involves volcanic products that are harnessed to create a renewable, clean energy resource. In Iceland, 45 percent of their energy comes from geothermal sources, and 87 percent of all their buildings are heated with geothermal water. Iceland sits atop a belt of active volcanoes—as do many other countries.[3]

It's hard to think of active volcanoes in beneficial terms, especially if you've suffered a loss because of one. But if you ask any geologist about a volcano's destructive force, you will also hear about the positives. Even as volcanologists insist on education about dangers, they are quick to profess their love for what they do. And once a volcanologist, it seems . . . always a volcanologist. As Carolyn Driedger put it, "We 'gray-hairs' keep on practicing the science because we love it so much."

Many of those who were at Mount St. Helens in 1980 found ways to pay forward their experience of escaping tragedy there. Sharing what they learned has been a driving force behind their passions and their careers. Dan Miller went on to lead VDAP for many years. Richard Waitt has worked at the CVO for decades; he wrote a book based on reports from hundreds of eyewitnesses to the eruption, and in it he explained the science as only a volcanologist can.

Tom Casadevall did a stint as acting director of the Geological Survey. He also received the 2006 Service to America Award for search and rescue work after Hurricane Katrina. He finished his career with USGS and entered the world of emeritus—which means he keeps traveling and working in the field . . . because he loves it.

Pete Lipman, whose life Dave dreamed of emulating professionally and personally, was asked to join the CVO when it was created. He declined; he didn't want the daily reminder of Dave's death, someone he'd considered a third son during their time together in Colorado. He said, "I've never gotten over losing Dave; I miss him." Pete finished his career with USGS but went back to the St. Helens area only a handful of times during almost four decades. In 2017, he attended the IAVCEI meeting in Portland and joined a field trip to St. Helens. He saw elk tracks among the hummocks, and ponds that were clear again; the return to life made him feel better about the area for the first time since the eruption.

Mindy Brugman talks of her passion for preparation for large earthquakes. She said, "The impact the eruption had on me is a lifelong quest to keep the public safer." And she admits feeling frustrated when efforts are slow or thwarted to put processes in place. Mindy once asked Don Swanson, "Why do I keep trying to get early earthquake warning? Did the eruption affect me that much?" He said that it likely did, and that it's okay to continue to stress what she sees as important because of her experience.

And Carolyn Driedger? She ended up at the David A. Johnston Cascades Volcano Observatory, where she has worked in public outreach for over two decades. Although Carolyn serves as a public information officer and outreach coordinator, she is first and foremost a geologist—a hydrologist to be exact. Hydrologic and eruptive hazards go hand in hand, as happened with the 1980 eruption. Carolyn's background means she is passionate about coordinating educational programs and working with local government when one of the Cascade volcanoes acts up.

Carolyn contributed to this book by providing a guided tour of the Mount St. Helens area, beginning with the CVO, which has moved twice since its inception. It now sits near the eastern city limits of Vancouver, which affords a view

Sign in front of the CVO. Photo courtesy of R. L. Holmes.

of Mount St. Helens about sixty miles in the distance. Nestled in a suburban tech park with tree-lined streets, the red-brick building houses seventy staff. That number swells to eighty-five in summer when graduate students conduct fieldwork and interface with CVO scientists.

In front of the building, a large black sign greets visitors: "USGS: Science for a changing world." The foyer is filled with publications and artifacts. There are various volcanic rocks, including one that erupted in August 1980—ejected during one of Mount St. Helens's smaller explosive eruptions.

Visible from the foyer is the hallway leading into the building with a painting of Dave; it is one that his parents had commissioned by an Oak Lawn artist. Next to the painting is a smaller framed photograph—the infamous "last picture" of Dave the evening of May 17, 1980. A camper is in the background, rocks surround him, evergreens tower in the distance. He sits in a folding chair, field logbook in his lap, pen in hand, feet propped on a log, and smiles for the camera. The picture has historical significance; however, Pat understandably prefers other images of her brother—ones where he isn't in the place where he died hours later.

Any tour of the CVO necessarily starts with the Seismic and Operations Room. "This room would pop Dave's eyes out," says Carolyn. It is the nerve center of the building with sixteen LED screens that surround a larger one. The screens are CVO's eyes—each connects to a webcam in the field that enables scientists to see what's going on throughout the Cascades—they can even see elk roaming.

In a lab, scientists explain that there are no commercial gas sensors that meet their needs; they need sensors that detect and measure different types of gases, so they build their own. CVO staff perform cross-training with scientists from other countries, teaching them to build the sensors. One such scientist was there the day of the tour, from Singapore.

In the Sediment Lab (Sed-Lab), a robotic arm can work with eighty samples at one time—the arm picks up a sediment sample, weighs it, records the result, places it back in its nook, then takes the next sample. It is more involved than this succinct summary, but that is the gist.

Sedimentation is the longest-lasting impact of an eruption. In the 1980 eruption, mudflows in the Toutle River eventually reached the lower Cowlitz and Columbia Rivers. The sediment decreased the depth of the Columbia River by twenty-five feet; river traffic was disrupted and ocean shipping choked closed. The Army Corps of Engineers dredged the Toutle, Cowlitz, and Columbia River channels to restore normal function—they removed enough material to build a twelve-lane highway from New York City to San Francisco.[4]

The main conference room is where press conferences are held. It's also where PhD candidates present their work. In 2016, Janine Krippner was there—one of a dozen students working with the CVO for the summer. Janine researched Shiveluch volcano in the Kamchatka region (the same region as Bezymianny); she compared the pyroclastic deposits of Shiveluch and St. Helens. Having grown up in New Zealand, a country with many volcanoes and frequent eruptions, Janine considers the chance to work with the 1980 deposits an "incredible honor."

A warehouse in the back of the CVO is filled with field equipment. There are three-legged "spiders" about five feet tall. Portable stations, they get their

182

Seismic and Operations Room. Photo courtesy of R. L. Holmes.

nickname from legs of stainless steel, widely spaced to help with stability in rocky terrain. A spider is a volcano-monitoring tool used at sites where ground crews can't work safely or where landing a helicopter isn't possible. Spiders house instruments in weatherproof cases that measure earthquakes, ground and glacier movement, gas emissions, and other tools that help detect potential hazards. Having this equipment prebuilt saves precious time—they can be quickly deployed in an emergency.

Next on the tour is the Johnston Ridge Observatory. During the almost two-hour drive from the CVO in Vancouver to the JRO, Carolyn points out the bridge that crosses Route 504 (also called Spirit Lake Highway) that delineates the beginning of the 1980 blast zone; it is fourteen land miles from the crater and thirty miles by road. When trees and other debris floated down the North Fork Toutle River and raised the level twenty feet above its banks, a bridge was photographed extensively as it was ripped from its foundation and floated away; where that bridge once stood is now a replacement.

At a stop-off along Route 504 in Kid Valley is a "sunken," or half-buried, A-frame house. Looking down into the interior through what was once a second-story window, the view is of the home's first floor. A refrigerator sits with its door hanging open; an electric stove with its burners popped out is nearby. In the back of the house, the second-story balcony is within reach, and a realization

View of Mount St. Helens's summit crater from JRO. Photo courtesy of
C. Driedger/USGS.

hits with full force—the ground surrounding the A-frame is lahar sediment from
1980, now grown over with grass and trees. Making the best of the new terrain,
the half-buried house is now a tourist attraction with an adjacent gift shop and
a statue of Big Foot out front. Tourism continues to be important to the area,
as it was in 1980.

At an elevation of 4,300 feet and five and a half miles from the volcano, the
JRO offers a mesmerizing view that attracts thousands each year. It is run by the
Forest Service, and staff are on hand to talk to visitors and show the documentary that repeats throughout the day. Once the film ends, the projection screen
rises and enormous drapes part, revealing a massive window that showcases the
mountain.

View from the JRO; jagged remnants of a tree in foreground. Photo courtesy of R. L. Holmes.

The facility is filled with exhibits. A plaque with a picture of Dave hangs on the wall; the inscription hails his dedication and enthusiasm for volcanoes.

Outside, people marvel at the mountain. In mid-June, snow blankets its flanks, crater, and dome. Bits of green push up through the soil, and purple and red wildflowers spread across the Pumice Plain. Clouds cover the summit, but they eventually subside, and the crater, with its growing lava dome, comes into view. Two separate domes formed during its eruptive stages in 1980–86 and 2004–8. They have since merged into one large dome.

"Magma is recharging," says Carolyn; which means magma is rising underneath Mount St. Helens, heaving the edifice upward once again. Mountains have collapsed and rebuilt themselves throughout history. Through future eruptive stages, Mount St. Helens will likely again become the beautiful peak aboriginals called Loowit. As magma recharges, USGS closely monitors its reconstruction.

Four billion board feet of timber were blown down by the directed blast; enough to build 300,000 two-bedroom homes. Old-growth trees were snapped and lay in an angled fashion away from the volcano. Next to the JRO, tree trunks with jagged tops are remnants of the eruption; they lack the smooth buzz cut of trees felled by man.

Some visitors come to pay their respects to Dave—one such visitor was "one of the guys" Dave grew up with in Oak Lawn, Illinois—Rich Batson. Rich described his reaction upon seeing the volcano as "subdued." He spoke wistfully about the group of boys who hung out together on the same block in Oak Lawn and the memorials that now exist for three of them.

The JRO is a visitors center, but it is also a sanctum of sorts. For those who lost loved ones in the eruption, and for those who have their own mountains to conquer, it is a peaceful place for reflection. "I still go there and pray," said Mindy Brugman.

The writing of this book opened the door for Carolyn to speak with Dave's sister Pat for the first time; they did so by phone in July 2016. For decades, Pat hadn't known her brother sent Carolyn and Mindy away from the ridge the night before the eruption; the facts weren't hidden but Pat avoided sources that might have revealed this information. During that call, Carolyn got to tell Pat about her brother's actions. Pat was overcome with gratitude and expressed how much it meant to hear her words.

A year later, Pat met Mindy. A film company was making a miniseries and they wanted to include people who were at Mount St. Helens in 1980. They offered to fly Mindy to Chicago to tell her story to Dave's family. Pat was the lone holder of the Johnston torch, and though she is camera shy, she agreed. She liked the idea of meeting Mindy, of course, but a big part of her willingness to participate was the chance to help create something to overshadow the movie that disparaged her brother's image in 1981. Pat had attended a school reunion months before the film company contacted her, and ex-classmates whom she hadn't seen in decades referred to the movie—they thought it represented reality. There it was again—that movie. So for anyone who doubts how much the Johnstons were hurt by how Dave was portrayed, picture an extremely nervous Pat just before the documentary began filming, doing what she could to set the record straight.

As for Carolyn, she and Pat finally met via Skype in early 2018—a quasi-face-to-face moment. Carolyn told Pat, "Dave was a testament to boldness. The way he spoke about his convictions inspires me." Then Carolyn put her hand on her own shoulder, and with a catch in her voice she said, "Sometimes I feel like he's right here—on my shoulder—when I speak to people about volcanic hazards."

Carolyn talked about the last night of Dave's life. It was a mostly upbeat evening before Dave asked them to return to Vancouver. Carolyn also described how Harry Glicken left Coldwater II in a jeep that night and coasted into town on gas fumes; then he broke the key off in the ignition. Harry was Harry, as people who knew him said with affection.

Pat and Carolyn Skyped for forty minutes, then they wished each other well. They look forward to a live meeting someday when Pat makes it back to the area.

Carolyn and her outreach teammate at the CVO keep busy transmitting information about volcanoes to public officials, land-use planners, emergency response organizations, news media, and the public. In June 2016, Carolyn was planning a meeting for those who live near Mount Rainier, a Cascade volcano considered one of the most dangerous in the country. When Rainier erupts, lahars will pour down its river valleys and entomb anything in its path. "Hundreds of thousands of people live in harm's way," said Mark Stewart, spokesman for Washington state's Emergency Management Division.

This is why CVO plans programs for all ages—from a camp-out for middle school teachers that enhances their ability to talk about the volcano with their students—to GeoGirls, which encourages geology and STEM* education—to a Boy Scout Volcanoree† with a fifteen-mile hike across St. Helens's debris field.

CVO's outreach programs ramp up each year in May, which is Volcano Preparedness Month in Washington. Creating disaster-resilient communities is the goal behind the annual communications push that coincides with the month of the 1980 eruption. They remind people that the Cascades volcanoes have erupted an average of twice per century over the past four thousand years and future eruptions are a certainty—it is always *when*, not *if* another eruption will occur.

---

* STEM stands for science, technology, engineering, math.
† Volcanoree is a play on the word jamboree; it's a large gathering of Boy Scouts or Girl Scouts.

Like having a fire escape plan, people who live near a volcano need to plan for the kinds of hazards that could strike—especially the ones that can occur with little to no warning. For those who live in a lahar zone, learning about evacuation routes in advance is crucial.

The internet affords opportunities that were not available just a few decades ago. For example, one way to receive alerts about volcanic hazards is through the Volcano Notification Service (VNS), an e-mail subscription service that sends alerts about activity at USGS-monitored volcanoes. For example, VNS generated an e-mail the day before the start of the 2016 World Series—the Chicago Cubs were playing the Cleveland Indians—as a volcano named Cleveland swung into action. Mount Cleveland is located on a remote and uninhabited island in the Aleutians of Alaska. As baseball fans went on heightened alert, so did the USGS. (Since Dave was from the Chicago area, it is noted here that like the Cleveland volcano that blew in 2016, the Cleveland baseball team followed suit; they blew it that year—the Cubs won the World Series for the first time since 1908!)

Why would you want to know about volcanoes that tremble and emit steam and ash on a remote island? Part of it is education. Understanding the number of hours devoted to monitoring these hazards makes for an informed citizen. Most important is that notifications reach governmental bodies who need the information—such as the Federal Aviation Administration, responsible for restricting air travel near volcanoes that exhibit a heightened state of unrest. An eruption at Redoubt Volcano in Alaska in 1989 nearly caused a commercial jetliner to crash when it flew through the volcano's ash cloud and experienced a complete failure of all four of its engines.[5] The airplane glided from 25,000 to 12,000 feet in eight minutes before the crew was able to restart two of the engines and land at Anchorage; no one was hurt but the "sandblasted" airplane was removed from service and the 231 passengers and 14 crew continued their flight to Tokyo on a different jet. A similar incident happened in 1982 due to ash that erupted from an Indonesian volcano.

Education and communications about volcanoes are crucial—a statement backed up, repeatedly, by history.

THAT MAN IS A SUCCESS WHO NEVER LACKED
APPRECIATION OF THE EARTH'S BEAUTY.

Robert Louis Stevenson

MEMORIALS WITH ROOTS

THE BEST MEMORIALS BRIM WITH LIFE. While Dave's friends and colleagues honored him in the areas where he worked, lived, and went to school just before he died, back in Oak Lawn he will forever be the Illinois boy who biked and ran along its streets.

From the time the Johnstons had put down roots in the village through 1980, Oak Lawn had grown fivefold. Still, residents heard of its native son who died on a mountain ridge over two thousand miles away. There was a new building going up for the local baseball league and the Oak Lawn Park District's board decided to name it for Dave.

Tom Casadevall traveled to Chicago, his second trip to Oak Lawn within a few months, and served as guest speaker for the dedication ceremony in September 1980. The building was dubbed the David Johnston Community Center.

Tom Johnston talked of hearing neighborhood kids say they were going to the Johnston Center to play ball, and said at the time, "We're very proud. Of course, there was a price to pay—but we've already paid the price."[1]

While the main purpose of the building is to support the local baseball league with its numerous fields, many others have put the "community" into the place

David Johnston Community Center, Oak Lawn, 2016. Pear tree planted for Dave in the foreground. Photo credit: M. Holmes.

in Oak Lawn that bears Dave's name. Boy Scouts have pledged their oath of honor there and it's been a teen center. Also, for many years the building was a pick up and drop off place for the navy's Adopt-a-Sailor Holiday Program. The park district transported sailors from the naval base in North Chicago, most of whom were far from their own homes, to the Johnston Community Center so that local families could share a meal with them—usually for Thanksgiving or Christmas.

Alice and Tom had made a request when the building was dedicated—one possibly inspired by a geologist's statement. In the weeks after Dave died, the Johnston home filled with letters, cards, and phone calls. One call came from a geologist from Champaign, Illinois—the location of Dave's alma mater—who told Tom that he didn't know Dave but he knew of his work and respected him.

Then the geologist said, "All good rocks come to the surface sooner or later, and when David comes to the surface he will be a tree."[2]

Alice and Tom asked the park district to plant two flowering pear trees near the Johnston Community Center. Almost four decades later, the trees still grace its entrance—the park district's horticulturist calls the trees ancient from the standpoint of their expected life cycle. One pear tree is a Chanticleer, a cultivar native to Vietnam.[3] A short distance from the Johnston Center is a memorial for Oak Lawn residents who died in military service, and on the list of fifty-two who make up the Gold Star Roll of Honor are Dave's childhood friends John Baird Jr. and Kenneth Gooley.[4] A tree that is native to Vietnam, planted to honor

Dave, does double-duty as a tribute to his friends. One can imagine strong winds carrying fallen tree leaves from the Johnston Center to the memorial for those fallen soldiers.

Though Dave's family could no longer feel the warmth of his embrace, they saw his passion all around—parks, stars, rocks, and of course, trees. A tree is a kind of poem whose leaves speak if you listen. Many more poems were planted in Dave's name—two trees were planted in a park in Tel Aviv, about six hundred miles short of the exact opposite side of the world from Mount St. Helens.[5] And a memorial grove of trees in Cowlitz County, Washington, whispers soothing sounds and stands sentry over a plaque with fifty-seven names.

Memorial rock and trees on grounds of USGS office. Photo courtesy of Jim Lewis.

Two more trees were planted in Menlo Park, California, where Dave had lived and worked. On the grounds of USGS– Menlo Park, a tree towers over the David

Plaque on David Johnston Memorial Rock, USGS–Menlo Park. Photo courtesy of Jim Lewis.

Johnston Memorial Rock and a storyboard explains the rock's journey. Called a bread-crusted block, the rock descended from the southwest flank of Mount

St. Helens between 450 and 500 years ago, from the pre-1980 summit. Formed of molten lava, the rock's interior continued to expand after it solidified; cracks formed at the surface and took on features of the crust on a loaf of bread.

A second tree was planted for Dave in Menlo Park—a gingko in Burgess Park.[6] The park is near the USGS office, thus, he would have run past it on numerous occasions. Burgess Park's setting is one of beauty, families, and nature. It has baseball fields and tennis courts—two sports Dave enjoyed in his youth. His diary speaks of a day long ago when he, his dad, and his sister played tennis . . . in the rain. They dodged raindrops and puddles and had "great fun."

Memorials can also be built of language. Emotions are the brick and mortar that form a monument in our hearts. Many people poured words about Dave into a concrete mixer that formed an image of the man they knew.

A handwritten, unsigned tribute is tucked inside the front cover of one of the four large binders compiled by Dave's parents. The poem was placed directly behind Alice's own handwritten speech (the one she gave at the CVO's dedication), which emphasizes its importance to the family. It sounds like the words of a parent, but it was penned by Dave's high school friend Jim Newquist. It took thirty-eight years to track down the poem's author, but the path led not to Jim, not to his wife, but to his daughter Alyson, because her parents have both died. Alyson recognized her dad's handwriting and told how her name would be David if she'd been born a boy in September 1980. The 1967 Richards High School yearbook includes a picture of the cross-country team with Dave standing next to their coach, Willie May, and the boy in the middle of the group is Jim. Following is Jim's poem, which sums up so much.

GOOD FRIEND

> We are here but an instant in time.
>> Sometimes the moment roars.
> Caught in emotion, we wonder,
>> What could have been?
> Steam, and gas, and fire
>> cannot remove the gift of you.

I knew you as a child,
    playing, running, laughing.
I knew you as a man,
    striving, achieving, living.
I knew you as a son,
    caring, believing, loving.

Your thoughts are with me now,
    and forever you will live.
The lesson that is your life
    continues to grow in me.
"Love life! Respect all things!
    Have hope."

Good friend, Dave,
    We walk the same path.
Goodbye for now,
    My life was blessed
for the pleasure of knowing
    you.

Legacy is more than that which we see. It's about inspiration that continues today. Dave was a hero who walked among heroes, all of whom deserve honor.

TO GIVE ANYTHING LESS THAN YOUR BEST IS
TO WASTE THE GIFT.

Steve Prefontaine

EPILOGUE

"I READ UNCLE DAVID'S DIARY YEARS AGO. It was like reading about an ideal childhood. He seemed naive and innocent . . . free of what I'd associate with being a teenage boy." This assessment came from Pat's son David. Some might agree, since fifteen-year-old Dave Johnston said "aww" and "gee" rather than expletives; he was a Boy Scout past the midpoint of high school—something uncommon in today's world when "cool factor" reigns at that age; and his young life definitely had its model aspects. He came from a loving, middle-class family with a home in the suburbs. He started a part-time career as a photographer during high school, and he had a plan for college.

Dave Johnston was in his midtwenties when he reread the diary he left at his parents' Oak Lawn home. In it, he saw himself as "a sweet young boy who wrote awkward, innocent lines full of self-doubt, fear, love, anger, and curiosity." Thus, uncle and nephew agree on the "innocent" part; however, if we read carefully, we see a world-weary teenager. Dave struggled with self-esteem and anxiety, just as many teenagers do today. But there was more; as the youngest and smallest, Dave pushed himself hard, perhaps harder than he had to. Also, the specter of Vietnam loomed, with reminders in the form of sonic booms made by jets that soared overhead.

At this writing, Dave and Harry Glicken are the only two American volcanologists to have died in eruptions. Others have died due to accidents in the field. Volcanologists from other countries have died in eruptions. Thousands living near volcanoes have died. Dave and Harry share this bond in death, but it is their *lives* that we focus on.

Both men were young and brilliant. Both advanced the understanding of hazards that threaten those who live or work close to volcanoes. In doing so, both lived lives in the pursuit of serving a greater good.

Like Dave, Harry was his parents' only son. His sister Anne talked to me in 2016 about her only brother, who graduated from Venice High School in west Los Angeles and went on to Stanford. She said Harry sought counseling and antidepressants to relieve survivor grief. And like Pat, Anne thought for decades that Harry asked Dave directly to cover Coldwater II the night before the eruption. Neither knew about Don Swanson's role; they had missed this fact despite its being available from various sources over the years.

Anne emphasized that Harry's motivation in his work was *to make the world a safer place*. He performed his work on the rockslide–debris avalanche process as a grad student, and he had hoped to be hired by the USGS. But by the time he completed his doctorate, a federal hiring freeze meant he had to look elsewhere. This is how he ended up in Japan on a postdoc. He was making the best of his situation.

Harry's sister and mother went to Tokyo for a memorial. "His friends told us that he was finding peace with himself," said Anne. "I wish he'd have been able to enjoy that peaceful part of his life for longer." Perhaps Harry's comment about what he wanted to do in retirement epitomizes his worldview—he wanted to write "funny volcano stories." Harry found the humor in life, even amid turmoil.

Dave's contemplation of his own early death when he was fifteen—from circumstances beyond his control—is perhaps not as unusual as one might think. After all, humans are the only animals that know they will die someday. Of course his comments about dying in the field are understandable within context—he worked at a time before certain safety protocols were put in place for fieldwork, such as issuing the right gun to handle a bear on the attack or establishing guidelines *against* heading to a volcano when there is cloud cover (as happened at Augustine in 1976).

Dave also contemplated the future. He saw himself outliving his parents and expressed to his sister that he would someday like to have just two things that belonged to their dad. If father had passed before son, Dave wanted his dad's World War II medals and his pestle and mortar (used by chemists)—symbols of courage and of science.

Although his family took comfort in the fact that he died in a place where he wanted to be, while pursuing his passion, they certainly didn't want him to perish there. No one wanted to lose Dave that way. Yet he experienced great joy and found love and fulfillment during his lifetime. Surely that is the measure of peace he would want them to hold onto. And perhaps he'd want people to embrace the humor, even the absurdity, of life—one of the items Dave had carried while working at St. Helens that found its way back to his family was the toy dinosaur he brought into a staff meeting.

"I'm sure Dave saw it and thought it was the funniest thing," said Pat.

Would Dave find humorous irony in the newspaper spread that juxtaposed an article about the first anniversary of his death alongside a picture of a dinosaur on a parade float? Perhaps.

Hey, he might say, *look around and find reasons to smile* . . . and of course, *Carpe diem!*

THE FACTS OF A LIFE ONLY HINT AT A LIVING,
BREATHING HUMAN BEING.

Terese Svoboda

AUTHOR'S NOTE

WE EXPECT OUR HEROES TO BE SAINTS. We romanticize their lives and don't want to hear that they got mad at their grandmother or that they called some curmudgeon a horse's ass. There may be people who will want to highlight things that I purposely left out to avoid unnecessary drama—there's been a lot already and the Johnston family (and others) have been through enough. My hope is that no one will feel compelled to shout their version of the truth—for what is truth really? Sometimes we can only brush against it. There was no reason to introduce certain topics, though I know of them, because life is this strange and wonderful, sometimes heartbreaking experience that we try to make the best of.

Dave professed at twenty-two that he dreamed of a life and a wife and kids like Pete Lipman's. In the days before he died, there were discussions, without timelines, without laying claims. Still, Alice went to her grave with the idea that her son had a plan to realize the personal part of his dream-life. Perhaps this thought helped Alice navigate the roiling river of what-ifs.

One of Dave's favorite songs when he was in his twenties was John Denver's "Annie's Song," which praises mountains and oceans and forests. During a period of Dave's life with an ongoing hot-and-cold romantic relationship, perhaps Denver's words resonated—lyrics ask about loving me . . . and letting me love you again. And then there are the lines about giving my life to you and dying in your arms. And we ask: Did the words resonate because of a woman or a volcano? Or was it just a song about nature that brought him joy? No one knew Dave's heart but Dave.

A number of tragic coincidences surfaced while I researched Dave's background. When Pat told me three decades ago that her family lived in Oak Lawn when the notorious killer tornado hit and that her brother later perished in a volcanic eruption, I silently wondered, *What are the odds of surviving one brush with a natural disaster only to die in another?* Then there are the two children whom Alice and Tom lost—a daughter and a son—in both cases the science didn't exist to save them.

The sad happenstances continued. Dave escaped Augustine Island just before the volcano erupted, then died at St. Helens. He took many calculated risks as a volcanologist, yet the event that took his life happened during his only shift at Coldwater II. Then Harry, who would have been in Dave's place if not for random circumstances, went on to die in a different eruption.

Also, images of the 1967 tornado and 1980 eruption are hauntingly similar. Bodies entombed in cars. Rescuers combing through the debris for survivors. Trees snapped or yanked from the ground. And forty-eight hours after the tornado, several inches of snow fell, which brought a ghostly aura to the devastated area, as with snowflakes of ash that fell after the eruption.

Three natural disasters hit one family. Different places. Different cataclysms. The results were the same in two of the three—neither Dave nor his Uncle Artie were found.

Doing justice to someone's life by telling their stories is a great honor. It's also a little scary to set down the words that tell the tale of a man, a family, a generation, and a career that is not well understood. Decades passed between the eruption and completion of this book, and it was challenging to reconcile various accounts of what happened. One preeminent volcanologist told me *not* to believe everything I read (he was spot-on). Pat passed along a maxim of her mother's: "Check a fact, then check it again." Alice's words still ring in my ears. Writing this book has been one of the greatest privileges of my life and it has changed the way I look at the natural world—from the lava rock that surrounds my home to pumice for self-care to granite buildings that line big-city streets that come from, in the words of a volcanologist, "a magma chamber that never realized its dreams because it never erupted."

My computer saw tears as I researched those killed at Mount St. Helens, Unzen, Galeras, and other volcanoes, as well as those who were struck down in lethal tornadoes and in hellish wars. Then there were the injustices suffered by those who traversed the hero's journey for civil rights. All these moments in history were visited during the writing of this book. Stories that still the soul into quiet awe.

At times, visions of Dave as a blond, energetic, lean guy, morphed into Pat's sons and my sons, two of whom turned thirty shortly after we began having bimonthly dinners to discuss her brother. Other times, my "sister hat" materialized and I thought of my own big brother who also died too soon.

Pat's son David wondered why his grandparents Alice and Tom collected and kept every letter and newspaper article about their son's death. He thought perhaps putting it out of their minds might have been better. Did they hope a book would be written about him someday, one that would overshadow the movie that hurt them deeply? Or was it their way of writing their own book of their son's legacy? Either way, I am humbled to have put words to the story that waited almost four decades to be told. To Alice and Tom, here it is; I hope you would have approved.

I close with a word about Pat. She mentioned a song artist to me from the 1970s who died in his twenties—Nick Drake. She mentioned Drake three times before I finally googled his song that she said resonated with her—"Fruit Tree." Drake's music didn't find a following until after he died, and in that song he seems to foretell that people will pay attention once you're gone. Like Drake, and I think this is Pat's point, Dave was talented, with a lot to offer the world, and these facts became known by "all" after he died. If he hadn't perished in 1980, there wouldn't be buildings named for him and students wouldn't pine for research funds that bear his name. The honors and memorials and comments that recall how Dave's hunches were right, it all sort of pales when what Pat really wants is a hug from her big brother. She believed in him; she listened when he spoke of an imminent eruption a week before he died. It took his death for the world to notice that which he spoke quietly about to his sister that day. Though no one can say what could have been done differently, these words ring true—we are so very sorry.

NOTES

CHAPTER ONE. TORNADO!

1. "Forty-Nine Years Ago Today: Infamous Blizzard of '67 Paralyzed Chicago," CBS Chicago, January 26, 2016, http://chicago.cbslocal.com.

2. Jim Allsopp, "40th Anniversary of Northern Illinois' Worst Tornado Disaster." NOAA, 2007. Author confirmed tornado still "worst" with Mike Bardou of NOAA, December 2016.

3. Lorraine Swanson, "Community Corner: 5:26 p.m., April 21, 1967," *Oak Lawn Patch*, March 10, 2016.

4. Victoria Pierce, "Tornado of 1967 Remains Indelible," *Chicago Tribune*, April 22, 2007.

5. Dirk Mooth, e-mail communication with author, September 30, 2016; original text from Oaklawntornado.com.

6. Oak Lawn Tornado Public Facebook Group, September 27, 2016.

7. "Voice of a Tornado," YouTube, www.youtube.com/watch?v=Nt6QGirpH40.

8. Pierce, "Tornado of 1967 Remains Indelible."

9. Kevin Korst, *Oak Lawn Tornado of 1967*, Images of America (Charleston, S.C.: Arcadia Publishing, 2014).

10. Timothy A. Coleman, Kevin R. Knupp, James Spann, J. B. Elliott, Brian E. Peters, "The History (and Future) of Tornado Warning Dissemination in the U.S.," *Bulletin of the American Meteorological Society / BAMS*, October 19, 2010.

CHAPTER TWO. THE JOHNSTON FAMILY

1. "The Arsenal of Democracy: Pullman Products During World War II," *Pullman Preservation Alliance*, www.pullman-museum.org/main/exhibits/pgtw/pgtw products.html.

2. Lorraine Swanson, "Hometown Celebrates Sixty Years of 'Modern Day Suburbia,'" *Oak Lawn Patch*, June 11, 2013.

3. Zay Smith, discussion with author, May 2016.

4. Obituary for Alice W. Johnston, *Chicago Tribune*, October 26, 2005.

5. Jan Barry, "When Veterans Protested the Vietnam War," *New York Times*, April 18, 2017.

CHAPTER THREE. YOUNGEST & SMALLEST

1. U.S. Department of State, *History of the Bureau of Diplomatic Security of the U.S. Department of State* (Westminster, Md.: Global Publishing Solutions, 2011), 122, www.state.gov.

2. "Teaching with Documents: Photographs and Pamphlet about Nuclear Fallout," National Archives, accessed May 4, 2016, www.archives.gov/education/lessons/ fallout-docs.

3. "Big Do in Toyland," *Tempo* 5, no. 16 (December 27, 1955), 11.

4. Caroline McClatchey, "Summer-Born Struggle: Why August Children Suffer at School," *BBC News Magazine*, November 1, 2011, www.bbc.com/news/magazine -15490760.

5. Maria Konnikova, "Youngest Kid, Smartest Kid?" *New Yorker*, September 19, 2013.

6. Ruth A. Wilson, "Belonging," *Exchange Magazine*, May/June 2012, www.childcare exchange.com.

7. Robert Peterson, "Marching to a Different Drummer," *Scouting Magazine*, October 2003, https://scoutingmagazine.org.

8. Mary Dearborn, *The Happiest Man Alive: A Biography of Henry Miller* (New York: Simon and Schuster, 1991), 33.

9. Katie McLaughlin, "Vietnam War: Five Things You Might Not Know," August 25, 2014, CNN, www.cnn.com.

10. Jim Banke, "NASA's Sonic Boom Research Takes Shape," November 6, 2013, www.nasa.gov.

11. Lefty Coaster, "How Duck and Cover Changed a Generation and They Changed America," Daily Kos, June 6, 2014, www.dailykos.com.

CHAPTER FOUR. COLLEGE YEARS & SHIFTING GEARS

1. Susan Katz Keating, "Nine Days in May," *VFW Magazine*, November 2004.

2. "Vietnam War Statistics," history-world.org/vietnam_war_statistics.htm.

3. D. L. Cade, "Photographer Mark Cohen and the Birth of Invasive Street Photography," June 4, 2013, https://petapixel.com.

4. Tjeerd H. van Andel and J. Brendan Murphy, "Timeline of the Development of the Theory of Plate Tectonics," *Encyclopaedia Britannica*, last modified April 18, 2017, www.britannica.com.

5. Robert Repino, "African Americans at Olympic Games," Oxford University Press blog, August 11, 2012, https://blog.oup.com.

6. Angela Jordan, "Black Power on Campus, 1968–1969," University of Illinois Archives, February 19, 2014, https://archives.library.illinois.edu/blog/black-power -on-campus-1968-1969/.

7. John D. Morris, "How Old Is the Earth According to the Bible?" *Institute for Creation Research*, February 1, 1995, www.icr.org.

8. Meg Jay, *Supernormal: The Untold Story of Adversity and Resilience* (New York: Twelve/Hachette Book Group, 2017), 67–73.

9. Peter Lipman, interview with author, November 2015.

10. J. Kienlie, Z. Kowalik, T. S. Murty, "Tsunamis Generated by Eruptions from Mount St. Augustine Volcano, Alaska," *Science* 236 (June 12, 1987), www.uaf.edu .cfos.

11. David A. Johnston, "Volcanistic Facies and Implications for the Eruptive History of the Cimarron Volcano, San Juan Mountains, SW Colorado" (master's thesis, University of Washington in Seattle, 1978).

12. "Augustine Reported Activity: January 22 to April 24, 1976," USGS Alaska Volcano Observatory, www.avo.alaska.edu.

13. Lee Fairchild, interview with author, April 4, 2018.

CHAPTER FIVE. STAGE FRIGHT

1. "Donny Osmond Confronts Panic," *48 Hours*, CBS News, February 24, 2000.

2. Bruce Britt, "Adele, Van Halen among Musicians Who Battle Stage Fright," The Grammys, May 15, 2017, www.grammy.com/grammys/news/adele-van-halen -among-musicians-who-battle-stage-fright.

3. Mayo Clinic, "Vasovagal Syncope: Overview," www.mayoclinic.org.

4. J. Croswell, D. Ransohoff, and B. Kramer, "Principles of Cancer Screening: Lessons from History and Study Design Issues," *National Center for Biotechnology Information*, June 2010.

5. Martha Hamilton, "The Costly Race to Replace CFCs," *Washington Post*, September 29, 1991.

6. "Chlorofluorocarbons and Ozone Depletion," *American Chemical Society*, last modified June 8, 2017, www.acs.org.

7. David A. Johnston, "Volatiles, Magma Mixing, and the Mechanism of Eruption at Augustine Volcano, Alaska" (PhD diss., University of Washington, 1978).

8. Chris Carlson, interview with author, January 2016; Gordon Brown, telephone communication with author, May 2016.

CHAPTER SIX. DREAM JOB

1. T. Kashdan, R. Sherman, J. Yarbro, and D. Funder, "How Are Curious People Viewed and How Do They Behave in Social Situations?" U.S. National Library of Medicine; *National Institutes of Health*, February 5, 2013, www.ncbi.nlm.nih.gov/pubmed/22583101.

2. "The Legacy of David A. Johnston," USGS, https://volcanoes.usgs.gov/observatories/cvo/david_johnston.html; Wes Hildreth, in discussion with author, December 2015.

3. Tom Casadevall, interview with author, November 2015.

4. David Johnson, "The Most Dangerous Jobs in America," *Time*, May 13, 2016.

5. Barry Voight, e-mail communications with author, September–October 2016.

6. Wendell Duffield of USGS to Johnston family, May 1980, and Barbara Jo Mueller of DOE to Johnston family, May 1980, Johnston family archives.

7. J. M. Carvalho et al., "Portugal Country Update 2015" (World Geothermal Congress, Melbourne, Australia, April 2015).

8. Marti Miller, interview with author, October 2017.

9. L. J. Patrick Muffler, "Donald E. White: A Biographical Memoir," *National Academy of Sciences*, 2016, www.nasaonline.org/publications/biographical-memoirs/memoir-pdfs/white-donald.pdf.

10. Darrell Herd to Johnston family, July 17, 1980, Johnston family archives.

CHAPTER SEVEN. FOLKLORE & HISTORY OF MOUNT ST. HELENS

1. C. E. Dutton, "Report on the Geology of the High Plateaus of Utah" (Washington, D.C.: Government Printing Office, 1880), 113.

2. Jose Viramonte, Jaime Incer-Barquero, "Masaya, the Mouth of Hell: Volcanological Interpretation of the Myths, Legends, and Anecdotes," *Journal of Volcanology and Geothermal Research* 176 (April 2008).

3. Kristine Harper, *The Mount St. Helens Volcanic Eruptions* (New York: Facts on File, 2005), 82.

4. "Native American Myths," *Volcano World*, Oregon State University website, volcano.oregonstate.edu/oldroot/education/livingwmsh/hr/hrho/nam.html.

5. Ibid.

6. "A Guide to Deciphering the Differences between a Yeti, Sasquatch, Bigfoot, and More," *Newsweek*, December 19, 2015.

7. Shirley Rosen, *Truman of St. Helens: The Man and His Mountain* (Bothell, Wash.: Rosebud, 1981), 81.

8. "Six Years Later Brian Ingram Gets a Piece of D. B. Cooper's Hijack Haul," *People*, June 23, 1986.

9. "George Vancouver," United States History, www.u-s-history.com/pages/h3710.html.

10. Dwight Crandell and Donal Mullineaux, "Potential Hazards from Future Eruptions of Mount St. Helens Volcano, Washington," USGS Bulletin 1383-C, 1978, https://doi.org/10.3133/b1383C.

11. Michael A. Clynne, David W. Ramsey, and Edward W. Wolfe, "Pre-1980 Eruptive History of Mount St. Helens, Washington," USGS Fact Sheet 2005-3045, 2005.

12. Michael A. Clynne, Robert L. Christiansen, Tracey J. Felger, Peter H. Stauffer, and James W. Hendley II, "Eruptions of Lassen Peak, California, 1914 to 1917," USGS Fact Sheet 2014-3119, December 2014.

13. James Irwin and Brandon Mercer, "Lassen Peak Began Years of Eruptions One Hundred Years Ago, Building to Massive Blasts and a National Park," KCBS/CBS Bay Area, May 29, 2014, sanfrancisco.cbslocal.com.

CHAPTER EIGHT. THE AWAKENING

1. Dwight Crandell and Donal Mullineaux, "Potential Hazards from Future Eruptions of Mount St. Helens Volcano, Washington," USGS Bulletin 1383-C, 1978, https://doi.org/10.3133/b1383C.

2. B. L. Foxworthy and Mary Hill, "Volcanic Eruptions of 1980 at Mount St. Helens; the First One Hundred Days," USGS Professional Paper 1249, 1982, https://doi.org/10.3133/pp1249.

3. Steve Malone, interview with author, November 2015.

4. Dave Johnston's media interview transcribed by the Film Loft; copy from Johnston family archives.

5. D. Frank, M. Meier, and D. Swanson, "Assessment of Increased Thermal Activity at Mount Baker, Washington; March 1975–March 1976," USGS Professional Paper 1022A, 1977.

6. "Geologist's Survivors Defend His Memory after the Latest Mount St. Helens Fallout: A Film Charging U.S. Cover-up," *People*, March 30, 1981.

7. C. Dan Miller, interview with author, September 2016.

8. Ibid.

9. Dick Thompson, *Volcano Cowboys* (New York: Thomas Dunne Books/St. Martin's Press, 2000), 52.

10. Foxworthy and Hill, "Volcanic Eruptions."

11. Ibid., 22.

12. Brian Howard, "Stunning Electric-Blue Flames Erupt from Volcanoes," *National Geographic*, January 30, 2014.

13. Barry Voight, e-mail communications with author, August 2016–April 2017.

14. Barry Voight's drawing in 1980 later appeared in his paper "Structural Stability of Andesite Volcanoes and Lava Domes," *Philosophical Transactions of the Royal Society*, May 2000.

15. Donal Mullineaux, e-mail communication with author, December 2016.

16. Tom Casadevall, interview with author, November 2015.

17. Richard Waitt, telephone and e-mail communication with author, October 5, 2016.

18. Richard Waitt, *In the Path of Destruction* (Pullman: Washington State University Press, 2015), 76.

19. Thompson, *Volcano Cowboys*, 78. Also as discussed with Johnston family.

20. Ibid., 69.

21. Foxworthy and Hill, "Volcanic Eruptions," 31.

22. Waitt, *In the Path of Destruction*, 66.

23. "St. Helens and Harry Truman Story," *Oregonian* video, www.youtube.com/watch?v=sST8GNEW0D8.

24. Shirley Rosen, *Truman of St. Helens: The Man and His Mountain* (Bothell, Wash.: Rosebud, 1981), 145.

25. Ibid., 131.

26. Waitt, *In the Path of Destruction*, 53.

27. Barry Voight, e-mail communications with author, April 2017.

28. C. Dan Miller, interview with author, September 2016.

29. Waitt, *In the Path of Destruction*, 87.

30. "Minute by Minute: The Eruption of Mount St. Helens," documentary, Tower Production for A&E Network, 2001, www.youtube.com/watch?v=fArB5Jz2wos. Swanson comment at 7:56.

31. Foxworthy and Hill, "Volcanic Eruptions."

32. C. Dan Miller, interview with author, September 2016.

33. Chris Carlson, interview with author, December 2015.

34. Carolyn Driedger, interview with author, December 2015.

35. Mindy Brugman, interview with author, December 2015.

36. Waitt, *In the Path of Destruction*, 103n8.

CHAPTER NINE. MAY 18, 1980

1. "1980 Cataclysmic Eruption," USGS, CVO Volcano Hazards Program, https://volcanoes.usgs.gov/volcanoes/st_helens/st_helens_geo_hist_99.html.

2. C. Dan Miller in Stephen M. Wessells, "Mount St. Helens: May 18, 1980," USGS, www.youtube.com/watch?v=A_77HLu8pBo.

3. Carolyn Driedger, discussion with author, June 2016.

4. Patrick Pringle, "Roadside Geology of Mount St. Helens National Volcanic Monument and Vicinity," Washington State Department of Natural Resources, Circular 88, 1993.

5. "1980 Cataclysmic Eruption."

6. T. Esposti-Ongaro, C. Widiwijayanti, A. B. Clarke, B. Voight, and A. Neri, "Multiphase-Flow Numerical Modeling of the 18 May 1980 Lateral Blast at Mount St. Helens," *Geology* 39, no. 6 (2011): 535–38.

7. Per USGS, as quoted in "Volcanoes and Climate Change," University of Washington College of the Environment, 2009, www.atmos.washington.edu.

8. "1980 Cataclysmic Eruption."

9. Sarah Sontag, "Always Ready: Eruption at Mount St. Helens," National Guard Association of the United States, May 18, 2016, www.ngaus.org.

CHAPTER TEN. AFTERMATH

1. Thomas Wright and Thomas Pierson, "Living with Volcanoes," USGS Circular 1073 (1992), 3.

2. Ibid.

3. Associated Press, "Volcanologist Reported Missing," May 21, 1980.

4. Tom Casadevall, interview with author, November 2015.

5. Theodore Roosevelt, "The Man in the Arena," speech delivered April 23, 1910, Sorbonne, Paris.

6. Ron Russell, "In Pursuit of Deadly Volcanoes," *Los Angeles Times,* June 25, 1991.

7. Department of Geological Sciences, San Diego State University, "How Volcanoes Work: Nevado del Ruiz, 1985," www.geology.sdsu.edu/how_volcanoes_work/Nevado.html.

8. Chris Newhall, e-mail communication with author, October 2016.

9. Chris Newhall, James W. Hendley II, and Peter H. Stauffer, "Cataclysmic 1991 Eruption of Mount Pinatubo," USGS Fact Sheet 113-97, https://pubs.usgs.gov/fs/1997/fs113-97/.

10. Bob Baugher, "Understanding Sibling Survivor Guilt," Open to Hope, November 23, 2008, www.opentohope.com.

11. "9-11: America Remembers," *Today Show,* NBC, September 11, 2013.

12. Steve Malone, telephone communication with author, November 8, 2016.

13. Don Swanson, telephone communication with author, November 20, 2015.

14. "The Taste of Death," *Columbian,* May 15, 2005.

15. Eric Johnson, "I Got to Sit on a Cliff and Feel the Earth Move," *KOMO News,* May 18, 2010.

16. "Survivors Recall 1980 Eruption of Mount St. Helens," *Chicago Tribune,* May 15, 2000.

17. A. Lynn, A. Cherry, C. Hill, "2005: Five Stories Unfold under an Ashen Sky," *News Tribune,* May 12, 2010, www.thenewstribune.com/news/speical-reports/article25858843.html.

18. "Weyerhaeuser Settles in Volcano Suit," UPI Archives, August 28, 1986, www.upi.com.

19. Erik Lacitis, "For Families of St. Helens Victims, Oso Brings Familiar Heartbreak," *Seattle News,* April 13, 2014.

20. Ibid.

21. Richard Waitt, communication with author, September 2016.

22. Public Papers of the Presidents of the United States: Jimmy Carter (1980), 952, https://books.google.com/books?id=WFbVAwAAQBAJ&dq.

23. Sam Savage, "Mount St. Helens Victims' Kin Sound Off," Red Orbit, May 18, 2005, www.redorbit.com.

CHAPTER ELEVEN. RECOVERY

1. "Geologist's Survivors Defend His Memory after the Latest Mount St. Helens Fallout: A Film Charging U.S. Cover-up," *People*, March 30, 1981.

2. *Mount St. Helens: Back from the Dead*, written, produced and directed by Nick Davidson ([Arlington, Va.]: distributed by PBS: NOVA6205, 2010).

3. Erin Middlewood, "Memorial Rite Recalls Day Etched in Minds: Anniversary of Mount St. Helens Eruption," *Oregonian*, May 19, 2000, www.freerepublic.com.

4. Jeff Renner, communication with author, October 17, 2016.

5. Bronnie Ware, *The Top Five Regrets of the Dying* (Carlsbad, Calif.: Hay House, 2011).

CHAPTER TWELVE. VOLCANOLOGY'S GIANT LEAP

1. Pat Pitzer, "The Overthrow of the Monarchy," *Spirit of Aloha*, May 1994, accessed April 2018, www.hawaii-nation.org/soatext.html.

2. "Goddess Pele Is Stirring," accessed December 2018, https://mountainmystery .com/2014/07/03/pele-stirring.

3. "Volcanic Hazards in the Cascade Range," USGS Project no. 97-60, March 25, 1969.

4. Peter W. Lipman and Donal Ray Mullineaux, eds., "The 1980 Eruptions of Mount St. Helens, Washington," USGS Professional Paper 1250, 1981, https://doi.org/ 10.3133/pp1250.

5. D. Swanson, T. Casadevall, D. Dzurisin, S. Malone, C. Newhall, and C. Weaver, "Predicting Eruptions at Mount St. Helens, June 1980 through December 1982," *Science* 221 (September 30, 1983).

6. Servando de la Cruz-Reyna and Martin Del Pozzo, "The 1982 Eruption of El Chichón Volcano, Mexico: Eyewitness to Disaster," *Geofísica Internacional* 48 (March 2009).

7. John W. Ewert, Marianne Guffanti, and Thomas L. Murray, "An Assessment of Volcanic Threat and Monitoring Capabilities in the United States," USGS Open File Report 2005-1164, April 2005. John Ewert confirmed via e-mail communication with author, October 2016.

8. C. J. Hickson and D. W. Peterson, "Special Symposium Commemorating Tenth Anniversary of Eruption of Mount St. Helens," *Geoscience Canada* 17, no. 3 (1990); Harry Glicken, "The Rockslide–Debris Avalanche of the May 18, 1980, Eruption of Mt. Saint Helens—Tenth Anniversary Perspectives," USGS Open File Report 96-677, 1996, https://pubs.usgs.gov/of/1996/0677/.

9. "Glaciation at Mount St. Helens," USGS, accessed December 2018, https:// volcanoes.usgs.gov/volcano/mount-st-helens/glaciation-mount-st-helens.

10. Donald Swanson, "The Observational Side of Volcanology," *Bulletin of Volcanology* 56, no. 2 (1994): 133.

11. Peter Baxter and Austin Gresham, "Deaths and Injuries in the Eruption of Galeras Volcano, Colombia, 14 January 1993," *Journal of Volcanology and Geothermal Research* 77 (1997).

12. John Ewert, phone and e-mail communications with author, October 2016.

13. Azadeh Tabazadeh and Richard Turco, "Volcanic Chlorine Emissions to Stratosphere," NASA, accessed April 23, 2018, https://geo.arc.nasa.gov/sge/jskiles/fliers/all_flier_prose/chlorine_tabazadeh/chlorine_tabazadeh.html.

14. "Ian Plimer's Volcano Claims Vaporize under Questioning on Australian TV," *Guardian*, December 16, 2009.

15. D. A. Johnston and J. M. Donnelly-Nolan, "Guides to Some Volcanic Terranes in Washington, Idaho, Oregon, and Northern California," USGS Circular 838, 1981, https://doi.org/10.3133/cir838.

16. Glicken, "Rockslide–Debris Avalanche."

CHAPTER THIRTEEN. TWENTY-FIRST CENTURY & BEYOND

1. Lee Fairchild, discussion with author, December 2015.

2. Erik Robinson, "A Race to Survive," *Columbian*, April 1, 2010.

3. Wendell A. Duffield and John H. Sass, "Geothermal Energy—Clean Power from the Earth's Heat," USGS Circular 1249, 2003.

4. "Hazards from Post-Eruption Excess Sediment at Mount St. Helens," USGS Volcano Hazards Program, https://volcanoes.usgs.gov.

5. "Mount Redoubt Volcanic Eruptions, March–April 2009," NOAA, January 2010.

CHAPTER FOURTEEN. MEMORIALS WITH ROOTS

1. Associated Press, "Geologist's Kin Delay Sad Visit," *Eugene Register Guard*, May 18, 1981.

2. Jean Fleszewski, "Young Scientist Died Doing What He Loved," *Suburbanite Economist*, May 28, 1980.

3. "Callery Pear Tree," Yale Nature Walk, Yale University, http://naturewalk.yale.edu.

4. Oak Lawn Veteran Memorial inscriptions: "L/CPL John R. Baird, Jr., USMC, KIA 2/22/69, S. Vietnam" and "PFC Kenneth R. Gooley, USA, 11/16/71, Chute Failure, USA." Ken Gooley died stateside during training for battle.

5. Associated Press, "Geologist's Kin Delay Sad Visit."

6. Tree planted in Burgess Park was a gingko per Johnston family and others; Menlo Park city arborist discussion with author, November 2016.

INDEX

MELANIE HOLMES graduated from St. Xavier University in Chicago. She is the author of *The Female Assumption*, recipient of a 2014 Global Media Award from the Population Institute. She is also a speaker, educator, and freelance writer.

The University of Illinois Press
is a founding member of the
Association of University Presses.

University of Illinois Press
1325 South Oak Street
Champaign, IL 61820-6903
www.press.uillinois.edu